D0570249

knits of a
feather

WITHDRAWN

knits of a feather

20 stylish knits inspired by birds in nature

by Celeste Young

SELLERS
PUBLISHING

Published by Sellers Publishing, Inc.
161 John Roberts Road, South Portland, Maine 04106

Visit our Web site: www.sellerspublishing.com
E-mail: rsp@rsvp.com

Design and layout copyright © 2013 BlueRed Press Ltd
Text copyright © 2013 Celeste Young
Patterns and templates copyright © 2013 Celeste Young
Photography by Celeste Young
All rights reserved
Design by Matt Windsor

No portion of this book may be reproduced, stored in a retrieval
system, or transmitted in any form or by any means, mechanical,
electronic, photocopying, recording, or otherwise, without the
written permission of the publisher.

The written instructions, photographs, designs, projects in this
volume are intended for personal, noncommercial use and are
protected under federal copyright laws; they are not to be
reproduced in any form for any other use.

ISBN 13: 978-1-4162-0913-3
Library of Congress Number 2013931248

10 9 8 7 6 5 4 3 2 1

Printed and Bound in China

Contents

Difficulty Key

Easy

Intermediate

Advanced

Knitting Needle Sizes	
METRIC SIZES(mm)	US SIZES
2.0	0
2.25	1
2.75	2
3.0	–
3.25	3
3.5	4
3.75	5
4.0	6
4.5	7
5.0	8
5.5	9
6.0	10
6.5	10.5
7.0	–
7.5	–
8.0	11
9.0	13
10.0	15
12.75	17
15.0	19
19.0	35
25.0	50

Introduction

My grandmother, Mary, opened up the world of knitting to me when I was just a child. Like many beginners, I made uneven scarves and misshapen sweaters for my dolls and bears. It wasn't until much later on, when I was in college, that I returned to knitting; that's when it became part of my life in a big way.

My college knitting club provided the perfect mental break from a heavy course load, and I wholeheartedly embraced it by knitting a cabled cardigan for my mother — and it fit! Delighted by this first success, I delved deeper into the craft, learning new techniques and meeting amazing friends in my knitting circle. In the meantime, I continued pursuing degrees in art history and education. But I found time to dabble in design, publishing patterns for a crocheted hat and tote bag.

Upon returning home to upstate New York, my good friend (and cover model!) Jessica took me to the new local yarn shop, Trumpet Hill. . . Fine Yarns & Accents. I immediately felt welcomed by the knitting community there, and the shop owner, Robena DeMatteo, invited me to try my hand at teaching. I have never been more terrified or exhilarated, but I instantly knew that teaching knitting was the dream job I had been looking for. Knitting is an incredible combination of art and math that I absolutely love, and I feel so fortunate to be able to put my training in education to work — to share my passion with my students and friends, and now, with you, my readers.

Knits of a Feather is my first book, and it is a celebration of the knitting styles and techniques that I cherish, all with a feathered twist! Birds are a plentiful source of inspiration for me, from their colorful markings to their stunning array of textures to their unusual patterns of flight. They symbolize grace and power, and after the long winter months, I always look forward to hearing their happy sounds — the first sign that spring is here. My projects reflect my great respect for their role in nature. The bright colors and strong angles of the Cardinal Cap (page 16) are an abstracted interpretation of its namesake, while I take a more literal approach to the Peacock Tam (page 10) and Bluebird On My Shoulder Cardigan (page 104). I have left plenty of room for interpretation in my designs so you can add your personal flair to them — choose your own color scheme for the Magpie Ring Pillow (page 122), go wild with feathers of every variety in the Feathered Shoulder Warmer (page 76), or continue increasing your Wingtip Shawl (page 80) into an oversized wrap. It is my hope that *Knits of a Feather* will introduce you to fun, new techniques and empower you to be creative as you make these one-of-a-kind knitted pieces. Write to me on my Web site, **CelesteYoungDesigns.com** — I can't wait to read about your results!

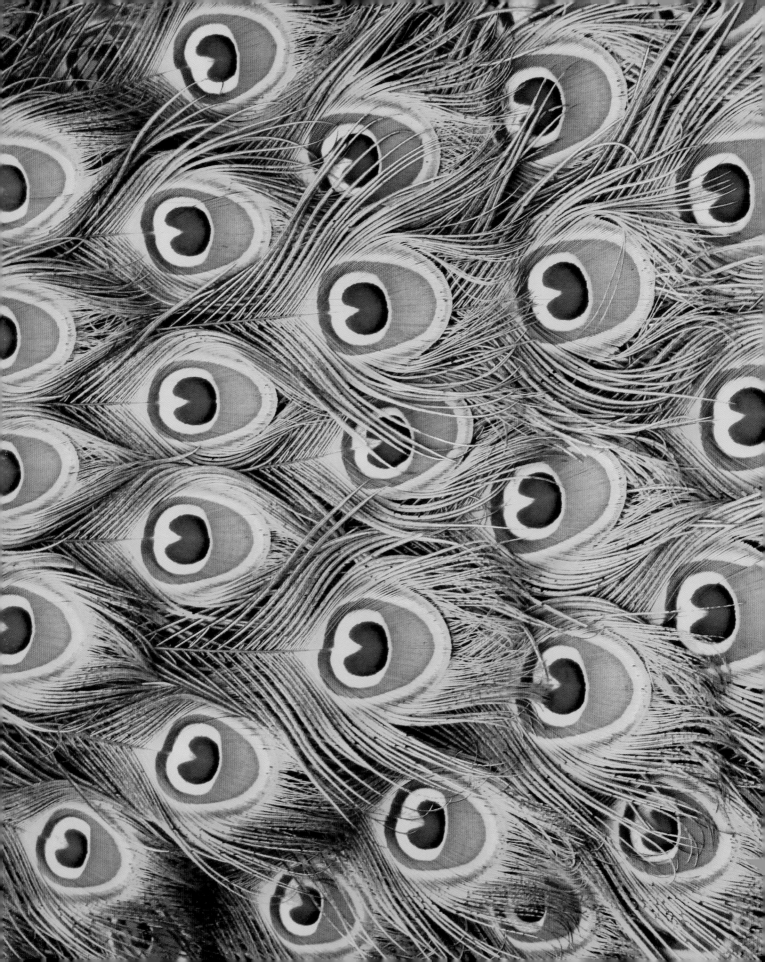

Hats

Peacock Tam

Delicate peacock feathers worked in stunning jewel tones wave around this lovely tam, knitted in fingering weight wool for light warmth and comfort.

Notes

- To avoid the problem of bi-colored purls, work the first round of ribbing in knit only.
- On longer runs of one color, catch floats of the unused color along the back of the fabric. Take care to catch floats in different places on each round to avoid the look of "gutters" on the right side.

Glossary of abbreviations

CC – contrast color

CDD – centered double decrease: slip next two sts together as if to knit, knit next stitch, then pass two slipped stitches over stitch just knitted and off needle.

CO – cast on

dec – decrease, decreasing

k – knit

m – marker, markers

M1 – make one increase: using left hand needle, pick up bar between stitches from front to back, then knit through the back of lifted strand to twist the new stitch and avoid a hole.

MC – main color

p – purl

rem – remain, remaining

rep – repeat

pm – place marker

RS – right side

sts – stitches

WS – wrong side

Finished Size

Designed to fit average woman's head (20–22" circumference). Tam measures 19" brim circumference unstretched, 10" high, 10.5" diameter after blocking

Yarn

Cascade 220 Fingering (100% Peruvian Highland Wool; 273 yd [250 m] 50 g): color 8393 Navy (MC), 1 skein; color 7813 Jade (CC), 1 skein.

Needles

Size 1 (2.25 mm) 16" circular, size 2.5 (3.0 mm) 16" circular and double-pointed

Notions

Tapestry needle, scissors.

Gauge

35 stitches, 36 rounds = 4" (10 cm) in stranded colorwork pattern on larger needles

Tam

Using smaller circular needles and long-tail method, CO 160 sts. PM and join to begin knitting in the round in corrugated rib pattern.

Setup round: using MC, k2; using CC, k2. Rep k2, k2 pattern alternating colors for one round.

Next round: using MC, k2; using CC, p2. Rep k2, p2 pattern alternating colors until brim measures 1.5" from CO edge.

Using MC only, work (k2, M1) around, picking up the navy strand between sts for each M1 (240 sts).

Change to larger circular needles and work rounds 1–81 of chart, moving to double-pointed needles when hat begins to dec and will no longer stretch comfortably around circular needles.

When chart is complete, 16 sts rem.

Cut yarn leaving a 12" tail and draw through rem sts twice. Take yarn to WS and secure.

Weave in all ends and block to finished measurements, stretching tam over a 10" dinner plate and placing plate atop a drinking glass to dry.

Step 1: To work CDD, slip next two stitches together as if to knit,

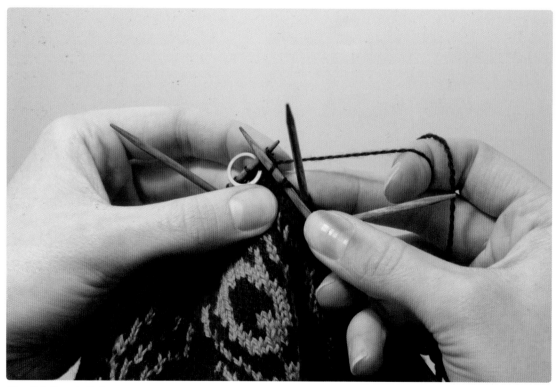

Step 2: knit next stitch,

Step 3: then pass both slipped stitches over and off.

Finishing: Draw yarn needle through remaining stitches, slipping stitches off of knitting needle and onto yarn needle as if to purl.

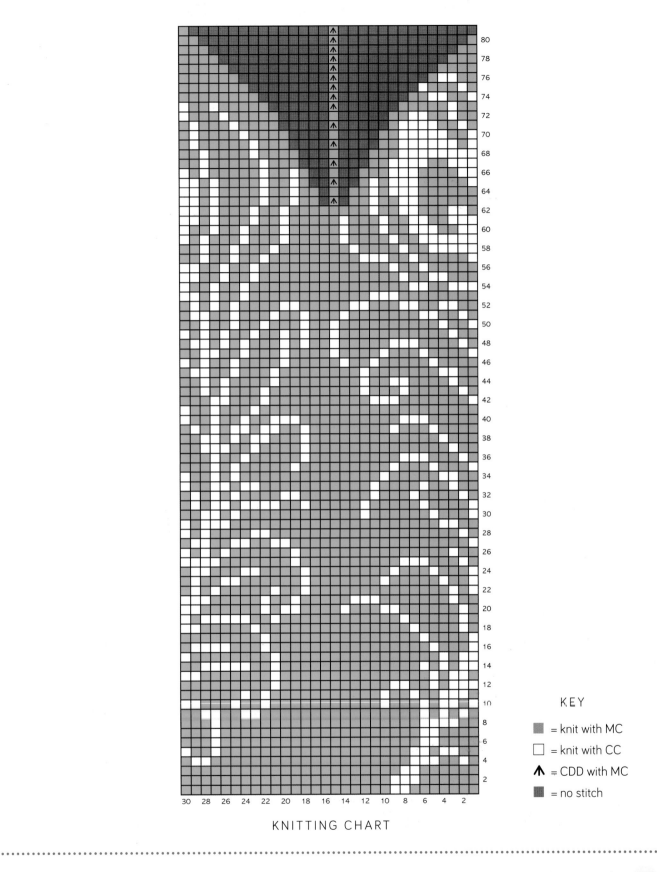

KEY

■ = knit with MC

□ = knit with CC

⋏ = CDD with MC

■ = no stitch

KNITTING CHART

Cardinal Cap

Knit the bold colors and striking markings of the cardinal in this sporty accessory! Choose traditional browns and red for the female cardinal, or red and black for the male cardinal. The unique shaping of this cap is achieved using short-rows, worked in ribbing and stockinette stitch and divided by a crisp, contrasting line of garter stitch.

Notes

- Cap is shaped using short-rows, worked by wrapping a stitch before turning work.
  To wrap a stitch in ribbing:
  - If the stitch just worked is a knit: slip next st as if to purl, bring yarn to front of work between needles, return slipped stitch to left hand needle, bring yarn to back of work between needles and turn. Yarn is in position to purl.
  - If the stitch just worked is a purl: slip next st as if to purl, bring yarn to back of work between needles, return slipped stitch to left hand needle, bring yarn to front of work between needles and turn. Yarn is in position to knit.
  To wrap a stitch in stockinette:
  - For wraps worked on the RS: With yarn in back, slip next st as if to purl. Bring yarn to front between needles and return slipped st to left hand needle. Bring yarn to back between needles and turn work. Yarn is in position to purl.
  - For wraps worked on the WS: With yarn in front, sl next st as if to purl. Bring yarn to back between needles and return slipped st to left hand needle. Bring yarn to front between needles and turn work. Yarn is in position to knit.
  To work a wrapped stitch:
  RS: put right hand needle into wrap first, then into stitch to be worked and work wrap and stitch together.
  WS: using right hand needle, lift wrap up onto left hand needle, then work wrap and wrapped stitch together.
- Directions are given for women's version first, with men's version in parentheses.

Glossary of abbreviations

beg – begin, beginning	pm – place marker
CC – contrast color	rem – remaining
CO – cast on	rep – repeat, repeating
dec – decrease, decreasing	RS – right side
k – knit	sl – slip
m – marker, markers	st, sts – stitch, stitches
MC – main color	st st – stockinette stitch
p – purl	WS – wrong side

Finished Size

Women's Cap: Designed to fit head sizes 19–22" circumference; finished cap measures 7.75" deep and 19" circumference (unstretched).
Men's Cap: Designed to fit head sizes 21–24" circumference; finished cap measures 8.5" deep and 21" circumference (unstretched).

Yarn

Cascade 220 Sport (100% Peruvian Highland Wool; 164 yd [150 m] 50 g): Women's Version: color 8013 Walnut Heather (Color A), 1 hank; color 9404 Ruby (Color B), 1 hank; color 8012 Doeskin Heather (Color C), 1 hank. Men's Version: color 8555 Black (Color A), 1 hank; color 8995 Christmas Red (Color B), 1 hank; color 9404 Ruby (Color C), 1 hank.

Needles

Size 4 (3.5 mm) 16" circular and double-pointed

Notions

2 stitch markers in different colors, tapestry needle, scissors

Gauge

25 stitches, 35 rounds = 4" (10 cm) in stockinette stitch

Cap

Using Color A, circular needles, and long-tail method, CO 124 (136) sts. PM and join to beg working in the round. Work in k2, p2 rib for 1 (1.5)", or 2 (3)" for folded brim. Maintaining established rib pattern, begin first set of short rows working in a flat, back and forth style:

Row 1 (RS): Work 59 (67) sts, wrap next st (second st of p2 pair), pm, turn. This "halfway" marker will act as a visual reference dividing the two "halves" of the short rows to come.

Row 2 (WS): Work 59 (67) sts back to beg of round, then continue past beg of round m in rib pattern to three sts before "halfway" marker. Wrap next st and turn.

Row 3: Work in rib back to beg of round, then continue in rib pattern to two sts before first wrapped st. Wrap next st and turn.

Row 4: Work in rib back to beg of round, then continue in rib pattern to two sts before first wrapped st on this "half." Wrap next st and turn.

Continuing in this manner, rep rows 3 and 4 until a total of 24 (28) sts have been wrapped (12 [14] on either side of "halfway" marker). When last st has been wrapped, complete the turn and end at beg of round marker. Cut A.

With RS facing, attach Color B and k one round, picking up all wraps and working them with their corresponding sts and removing "halfway" marker when you come to it. Purl 1 round, knit 1 round, purl 1 round. Cut B.

With RS facing, attach Color C and knit one round. Continuing in stockinette stitch, begin second set of short rows working in a flat, back and forth style:

Row 1 (RS): Knit 62 (70) sts, wrap next st and turn.

Row 2 (WS): Purl 2 sts, wrap next st and turn.

Row 3: Knit to first wrapped st, pick up wrap and work it with corresponding st, k1, wrap next st and turn.

Row 4: Purl to wrapped st, pick up wrap and work it with corresponding st, p1, wrap next st and turn.

Continuing in this manner, rep rows 3 and 4 until a total of 24 (28) sts have been wrapped, and 23 (27) wraps have been worked (one wrap remains). When last st has

Step 1: To work a wrapped stitch on the RS, put right hand needle into wrap first,

Step 2: then into stitch to be worked,

Step 3: and work wrap and stitch together.

been wrapped, complete the turn and knit back around to beg of round marker. Resume knitting in the round, picking up and working remaining wrap when you come to it. Work even in st st until cap measures 6 (7)" from CO edge, or 7 (8.5)" for folded brim option. Begin decreasing, moving to double-pointed needles when cap will no longer stretch comfortably around circular needles:

Women's Size Only:
Round 1: (K10, k2tog, k10, k3tog) 4 times, (k10, k2tog) 2 times.

Men's Size Only:
Round 1: (K10, k2tog, k10, k3tog, k10, k2tog) 3 times, k10, k2tog, k10, k3tog.

Both sizes:
Round 2: Knit.
Round 3: (K9, k2tog) 10 (11) times.
Round 4: Knit.
Round 5: (K8, k2tog) 10 (11) times.
Round 6: Knit.
Round 7: (K7, k2tog) 10 (11) times.
Round 8: Knit.
Round 9: (K6, k2tog) 10 (11) times.
Round 10: Knit.
Round 11: (K5, k2tog) 10 (11) times.
Round 12: (K4, k2tog) 10 (11) times.
Round 13: (K3, k2tog) 10 (11) times.
Round 14: (K2, k2tog) 10 (11) times.
Round 15: (K1, k2tog) 10 (11) times.
Round 16: (K2tog) 10 (11) times.
Round 17: K2tog 5 times, k 0 (1). Break yarn and thread tail through 5 (6) rem sts twice. Pull snugly, then take yarn to WS of work and weave in. Weave in all ends and block to finished measurements, using a head form as desired.

Feathered Cloche

A feather plume curls around the edge of this sweet knitted cloche. Classic gray and black add a dramatic flourish to any outfit, or choose your favorite color to make a bold statement!

Notes

- This hat is designed to be close-fitting and worn with 1–2" of negative ease. For example, if your head measures 23" around, choose the 22" size for a comfortable fit.
- Feather detail is embroidered using chain stitch technique once knitting is completed.

Cloche

CO 104 (112) stitches and pm; join to begin working in the round.
Round 1: Purl.
Round 2: Knit.
Round 3: Purl.
Rounds 4–9: Knit.
Round 10: (K6, k2tog) around (91 [98] sts rem).
Round 11: Knit.
Round 12: Purl.
Continue knitting in st st for 3.25 (3.5)", or until hat measures approximately 5.25 (5.5)" from CO edge. Begin spiral decreases, changing to double-pointed needles when necessary:
For 22" hat, begin dec rounds here:
Round 1: (K12, k2tog) around (91 sts rem).
Round 2: Knit.
For 20" hat, begin dec rounds here:
Round 3: (K11, k2tog) around (84 sts rem).
Round 4: Knit.
Round 5: (K10, k2tog) around (77 sts rem).
Round 6: Knit.

Round 7: (K9, k2tog) around (70 sts rem).
Round 8: Knit.
Round 9: (K8, k2tog) around (63 sts rem).
Round 10: Knit.
Round 11: (K7, k2tog) around (56 sts rem).
Round 12: (K6, k2tog) around (49 sts rem).
Round 13: (K5, k2tog) around (42 sts rem).
Round 14: (K4, k2tog) around (35 sts rem).
Round 15: (K3, k2tog) around (28 sts rem).
Round 16: (K2, k2tog) around (21 sts rem).
Round 17: (K1, k2tog) around (14 sts rem).
Round 18: K2tog around (7 sts rem).

Break yarn, leaving a 10" tail. Thread tail onto tapestry needle and draw through remaining stitches twice. Pull snugly, then take tail to WS of work and weave in. Block hat to finished measurements, then embroider feather detail referencing photos and embroidery illustration. Secure all ends once embroidery is completed, then re-block embroidered area as needed to smooth work.

Finished Size

Designed to fit head size 21 (23)"; finished hat measures 20 (22)" around.

Yarn

Cascade Sitka (80% Merino Wool, 20% Kid Mohair; 131 yd [120 m] 100 g): color 14 Grey, 1 hank
Cascade 220 Sport (100% Peruvian Highland Wool; 164 yd [150 m] 50 g): color 8555 Black, 1 hank (for embroidery detail).

Needles

Size 8 (5.0 mm) 16" circular and double-pointed

Notions

Stitch marker (m), tapestry needle, scissors

Gauge

18 stitches, 27 rounds = 4" (10 cm) in stockinette stitch using Sitka yarn.

Glossary of abbreviations

CO – cast on
dec – decrease, decreasing
k – knit
k2tog – knit two stitches together
m – marker, markers
rem – remain, remaining
rep – repeat
pm – place marker
st st – stockinette stitch
sts – stitches
WS – wrong side

CHAIN STITCH EMBROIDERY

Step 1: Setup: With RS of work facing, bring yarn needle from the back of the work to begin the first chain stitch. Insert the needle down into the same space and up again, approximately 0.25" away. Keep needle above the working yarn.

Step 2: : Slowly tighten, adjusting the shape of the chain stitch before beginning the next one in the same manner.

Note: To finish off a column of chain stitches, simply insert the needle down into the work and bring it back up where the next run of stitches will begin without catching the working yarn on the RS.

STITCHING CHART

Scarves & Cowls

Birds on a Wire Cowl

Birds encircle this cozy cowl, worked in warm sport weight wool yarn. Border it with bi-colored ribbing as pictured for a bold, graphic look, or single color ribbing for a more subtle effect!

Notes

- Cowl is worked in the round with RS facing throughout pattern.
- Position MC to be worked in the right hand, CC in the left hand. This will ensure that the CC appears dominant, allowing the birds to visually pop!
- Secure floats of unused color on WS of work every 5–6 sts, taking care to secure in different locations for each round to avoid gutters.
- On rounds using only one color, drop unused color and allow to hang at the back of work. Loosely carry it up on the WS to use again on later rounds. This will create a vertical float on the back of the work.

Stitch Guide

Corrugated Rib (multiple of 4 sts)
Round 1: *K2 in MC, p2 in CC; rep from * around.
Round 2: Knit the knit sts in MC and purl the purl sts in CC.
Rep round 2 for pattern.

Cowl

Using long-tail CO and circular needle, CO 156 stitches. Place beginning of round marker and join to begin working in the round.
Round 1: Join CC and begin working in corrugated rib pattern.

When preparing to knit with the color that has been resting, spread the stitches out wide on the right hand needle. This will prevent your floats from being too tight and puckering the fabric.

Finished Size

25" circumference, 7.25" deep after blocking

Yarn

Cascade 220 Sport (100% Peruvian Highland Wool; 164 yd [150 m] 50g): color 8401 Silver Grey (MC), 1 hank; Color 4002 Jet (CC), 1 hank

Needles

Size 6 (4.25 mm) 16" circular

Notions

3 markers (m), 2 of one color and 1 of another color to mark beginning of round, tapestry needle, scissors

Gauge

25 sts and 31 rows = 4" (10 cm) in stranded pattern

Glossary of abbreviations

CC – contrast color
CO – cast on
m – marker, markers
MC – main color
rep – repeat
RS – right side
sts – stitches
WS – wrong side

Rounds 2–9: Continue working corrugated rib pattern.

Round 10: Begin chart pattern, working three repeats around cowl. Place a marker after each repeat.

Rounds 11–45: Continue working chart pattern.

Round 46: Resume corrugated rib pattern, knitting all sts this round to avoid the problem of bi-colored purls: *K2 in MC, k2 in CC; rep from * around.

Rounds 47–54: Continue working in corrugated rib pattern, knitting and purling as before.

Round 55: Using CC, knit all sts around.

Bind off in CC and cut yarns. Weave in ends on WS of work and block to finished measurements.

SECURING FLOATS

Step 1: To secure the unused CC at the back of the work while using the MC, insert right hand needle into next stitch as if to knit. Lift CC up and onto the right hand needle, but do not knit with it.

Step 2: Keeping CC up on the right hand needle, yarn over with MC as if to knit normally. Now drop CC back off of needle. Knit next stitch as normal. Float has been secured!

Detail Secured Float: Close up view of float that has been secured to WS of work.

MARKER PLACEMENT

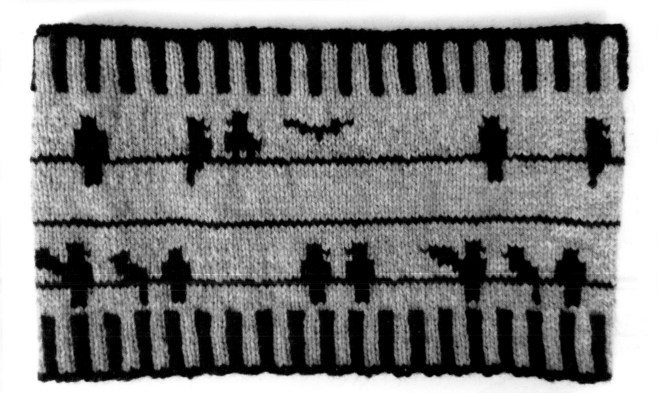

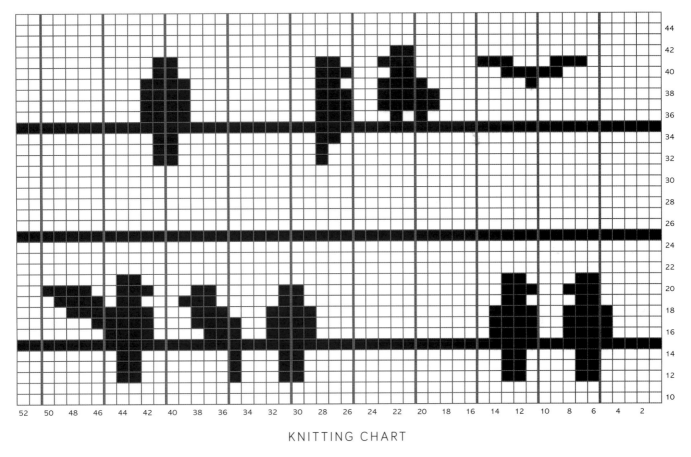

KNITTING CHART

KEY

 = k with MC

 = k with CC

Feathered Nest Cowl

A woven nest of cables to keep your neck warm and cozy! The luxurious blend of merino wool and baby alpaca in Cascade Cloud is every bit as comfortable and inviting as a real feathered nest. Choose the small size for a tighter, neck-hugging fit, or the larger size for a draped effect.

Notes

- Directions are written for smaller cowl, with larger cowl stitch counts in parentheses.
- Slipping first stitch of every row as if to purl creates a neat edge.

Cowl

Using crochet hook and waste yarn, chain 46 (70) stitches.

Working in back bumps of chain, use knitting needle and project yarn to pick up 44 (68) stitches for cowl as follows: skip first chain, pick up one stitch for each chain that follows, skip last chain.

Setup row (WS): Slip 1, p1, k2, pm, (p2, k2, p2, k4, p2) 3 (5) times, pm, k2, p2.

Begin chart, working 12 st repeat 3 (5) times between markers.

Rep rows 1–16 7 (10) times, then rows 1–15 once more.

Remove provisional cast on and return live sts to second straight needle.

Hold needles with right sides of cowl together, WS facing out. Using spare size 9 needle, work 3-needle bind off across all stitches using photos for reference. Weave in ends and block lightly to finished measurements.

Finished Size

Small Cowl: 8" high, 9.5" wide after blocking
Large Cowl: 10" high, 14.5" wide after blocking

Yarn

Cascade Cloud (70% Merino, 30% Baby Alpaca; 164 yd [150 m] 100 g): Small Cowl used color 2126 Chocolate, 1 hank; Large Cowl used color 2112 White, 2 hanks.

Needles

Size 9 (5.5 mm) straight

Notions

Cable needle, tapestry needle, scissors, smooth waste yarn of similar weight, size I (5.5 mm) crochet hook, spare size 9 (5.5 mm) knitting needle for 3-needle bind off

Gauge

18 stitches, 25 rows = 4" (10 cm) in stockinette stitch; 20 stitches, 26 rows = 4" (10 cm) in cable pattern

Glossary of abbreviations

cn – cable needle
k – knit
m – marker, markers
p – purl
rep – repeat
pm – place marker
RS – right side
st, sts – stitch, stitches
WS – wrong side

Small Cowl

3-NEEDLE BIND OFF

Step 1: Remove provisional cast on one stitch at a time, slipping newly released cowl stitches onto knitting needle as you go by inserting needle tip from back to front through each stitch.

Step 2: Hold knitting needles together with right sides of cowl together, WS facing out.

Step 3: Using spare size 9 needle, begin 3-needle bind off by knitting the first stitch from the front needle together with the first stitch from the back needle. Repeat for second stitches from front and back needles.

Step 4: Using one of the left hand needle tips, lift first stitch from right hand needle over second stitch and off, just as you would for a typical bind off. Repeat steps 3 and 4 until all stitches have been bound off.

Small Cowl (foreground) and Large Cowl (rear)

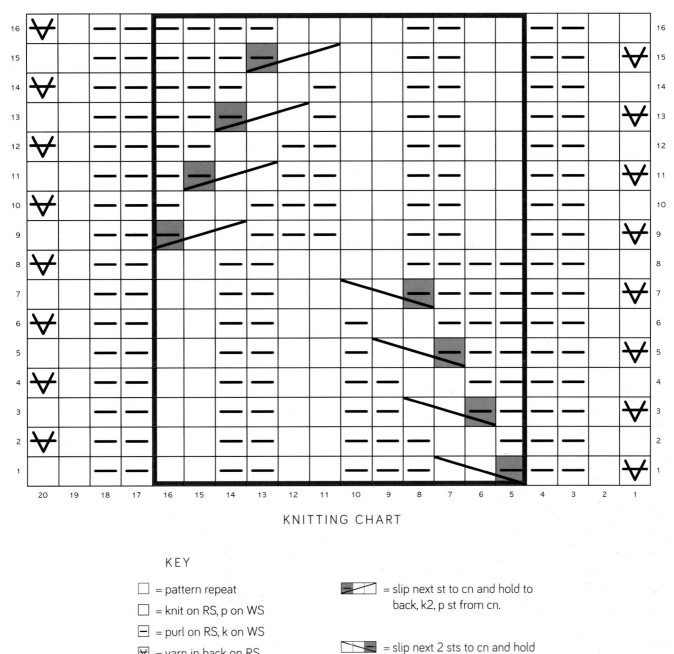

KNITTING CHART

KEY

☐ = pattern repeat

☐ = knit on RS, p on WS

⊟ = purl on RS, k on WS

⌄̵ = yarn in back on RS,
slip st as if to purl, holding
yarn in the front on WS

= slip next st to cn and hold to
back, k2, p st from cn.

= slip next 2 sts to cn and hold
to front, p1, k2 sts from cn

Sandpiper Scarf

The cheerful tracks of the sandpiper wave down the length of this sand-colored lace scarf, knitted in luxurious baby alpaca. A touch of feather and fan lace on each end is reminiscent of the morning tide flowing onto the beach.

Notes

- Scarf is knitted in two identical halves, then grafted together using kitchener stitch.
- Cast-on is worked using double thickness of yarn for added stability.

Stitch Guide

Stockinette Stitch

Row 1 (RS): knit.
Row 2 (WS): purl.

Scarf

Holding 2 strands together and using cable method, CO 69 sts.

Cut one strand to work scarf with single thickness and knit 6 rows.

Begin border chart: k3 sts for garter st edge, pm, work border pattern rep three times, pm, k3 sts for garter st edge.

Rep rows 1–4 of border chart six times, ending on a WS row.

Work 3 rows in st st, maintaining garter st borders.

Begin Sandpiper Tracks chart, working pattern rep 3 times across each row.

Rep rows 1–24 nine times.

Place sts on holder or scrap yarn and work a second identical piece, leaving second piece on the needles once complete.

Return held sts to empty knitting needle and hold scarf halves with WS together, RS facing out.

Graft live sts together using kitchener method. Adjust graft tension to match knitting tension. Weave in all ends and block to finished measurements.

Finished Size

Approximately 10.5" wide, 66" long after blocking.

Yarn

Cascade Alpaca Lace (100% Baby Alpaca; 437 yd [400 m] 50 g): color 1402 Camel, 2 hanks.

Needles

Size 6 (4.0 mm) straight or circular

Notions

Stitch markers, stitch holder or scrap yarn, tapestry needle, scissors.

Gauge

24 stitches, 32 rows = 4" (10 cm) in stockinette stitch after blocking

Glossary of abbreviations

CO – cast on
k – knit
m – marker, markers
pm – place marker
rep – repeat
RS – right side
st st – stockinette stitch
st, sts – stitch, stitches
WS – wrong side

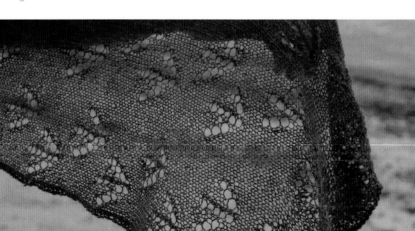

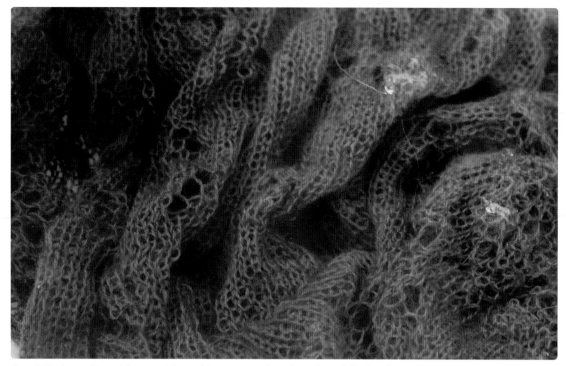

Step 1: Soak scarf in tepid water with a mild soap or wool wash as desired. Soak at least 30 minutes to ensure that the core of the yarn is saturated.

Step 2: Drain, then press out any remaining water. Gently lift scarf out of basin and lay on a towel to blot. Do not twist or wring!

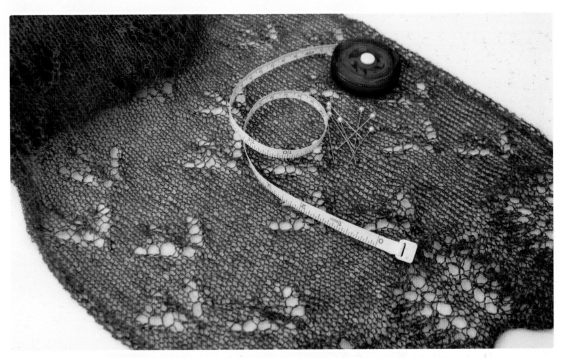

Step 3: Lay scarf on blocking surface (a rubber mat, vinyl tablecloth, or large towel will work well) with rust proof pins, measuring tape, and final measurements (see pattern) handy.

Step 4: Carefully stretch scarf to finished measurements, pinning approximately every inch and working from one end to the other. Measure periodically to ensure that the sides remain even and you are not over or under stretching the work, using finished measurements and gauge for reference.

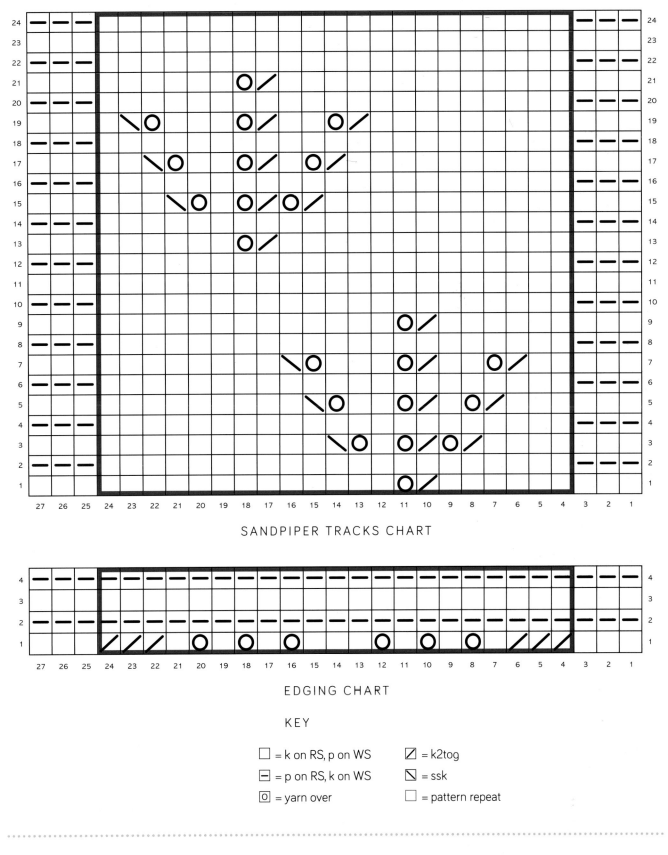

SANDPIPER TRACKS CHART

EDGING CHART

KEY

☐ = k on RS, p on WS

⊟ = p on RS, k on WS

□O□ = yarn over

╱ = k2tog

╲ = ssk

☐ = pattern repeat

Hands & Wrists

Robin's Egg Wristlets

Feather Beaded Cuff

Lovebird Mittens

Robin's Egg Wristlets

Bright and cheerful as a robin's egg, these wristlets are sure to draw attention! Warm up your stranded colorwork skills with a simple speckled chart. Superwash merino yarn makes a warm, practical choice for this hard-wearing accessory.

Notes

- Tighter tension in stranded colorwork is common. To accommodate this, consider using size 6 double-pointed needles for the charted portion of the fingerless mitts.

Glossary of abbreviations

BO – bind off
CC – contrast color
CO – cast on
dec – decrease, decreasing
k – knit
m – marker, markers
M1L – make one left increase: insert left hand needle under bar between stitches from front to back; knit through back loop.

M1R – make one right increase: insert left hand needle under bar between stitches from back to front; knit through front loop.
MC – main color
p – purl
pm – place marker
rep – repeat
RS – right side
sl – slip
st, sts – stitch, stitches
WS – wrong side

Finished Size

Designed to fit women's medium hand. Wristlet measures 7" circumference, unstretched.

Yarn

Cascade 220 Superwash Sport (100% Superwash Merino Wool; 136 yd [125 m] 50 g): color 818 Mocha (MC), 1 hank; color 849 Dark Aqua (CC), 1 hank.

Needles

Set of 5 size 5 (3.75 mm) double-pointed.

Notions

Three stitch markers, scrap yarn, tapestry needle, scissors

Gauge

24 stitches, 35 rounds = 4" (10 cm) in stockinette stitch

Wristlets

Using MC, CO 44 sts. Distribute onto 4 double-pointed needles, pm and join to begin working in the round.

Rounds 1–10: Work in (k2, p2) rib around.
Round 11: Knit.
Round 12: Join CC and begin chart. Work rounds 1–12 of chart, cutting MC when complete. Continue working in stockinette stitch using CC only for 5 more rounds.
Begin thumb gusset:
Round 1: K1, M1R, pm, knit to last st, pm, M1L, k1.
Round 2: Knit.
Round 3: Knit.
Round 4: Knit to marker, M1R, sl m, knit to next marker, sl m, M1L, k to end.
Rep rounds 2–4, working two rounds even

followed by one increase round until there are 8 sts before first marker (16 total thumb sts). Knit 1 round even.
Thread scrap yarn onto yarn needle and prepare to separate thumb stitches, using photos for reference: K to first marker, remove m and place 8 sts just worked onto scrap yarn. Continue knitting around to second marker, remove m and place next 8 sts (unworked) onto same scrap yarn.
Tie off to keep live thumb stitches secure. Using reverse loop method, CO 1 st, place beg of round m, CO 1 st (44 sts). Rejoin to continue working in the round.
Knit 9 rounds even, followed by 5 rounds in (k2, p2) ribbing. BO loosely in pattern.

Thumb

Return held sts from scrap yarn to three double-pointed needles. Leaving a 6–8" tail, join CC yarn at first st and k around all 16 sts, then M1R, pick up 2 sts in base of CO sts, M1L (20 sts).
Knit 5 rounds even, followed by 5 rounds in (k2, p2) ribbing. BO loosely in pattern.

Finishing

Weave in ends on WS of work, taking care to close any small holes that may exist at thumb divide.
Block gently to finished measurements.

Step 1: K to first marker, remove m and place 8 sts just worked onto scrap yarn.

Step 2: Continue knitting around to second marker, remove m and place next 8 sts (unworked) onto same scrap yarn.

Step 3: Tie off scrap yarn to keep live thumb stitches secure.

Step 4: Using reverse loop method, CO 1 st.

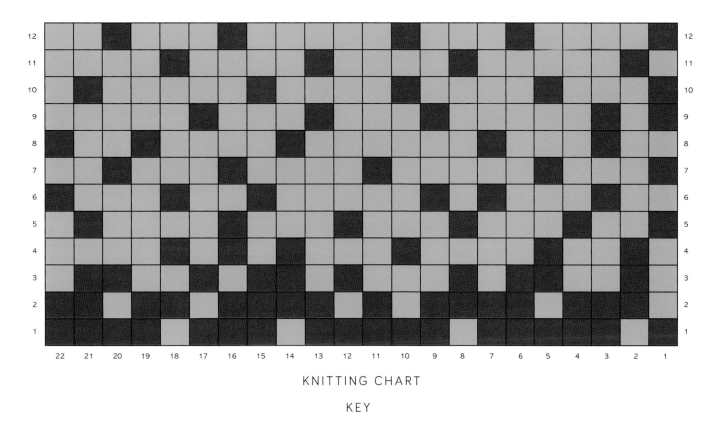

KNITTING CHART

KEY

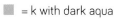 = k with dark aqua

= k with mocha

Feather Beaded Cuff

Symbolic of truth, speed, and the celestial realm, feathers have played a powerful role in numerous cultures and religions around the world. Keep a feather close at hand with this beaded cuff, knit from a luxurious blend of mulberry silk and merino wool.

Notes

- Bangle cover is knitted flat and seamed together around bangle.
- Beads are not pre-strung, but rather pulled into place using smaller crochet hook. Following the feather chart for placement, knit to bead symbol and then load 1 bead onto hook, slip knit stitch off left needle and onto hook, then slide bead off hook and onto knit stitch. Return stitch to left knitting needle and knit as usual.

Glossary of abbreviations

CO – cast on	pm – place marker
k – knit	RS – right side
m – marker, markers	sts – stitches
p – purl	WS – wrong side

Scarf

Using larger crochet hook and waste yarn, chain 30 stitches. Working in back bumps of chain, use knitting needle and project yarn to pick up 28 stitches for cuff as follows: skip first chain, pick up one stitch for each chain that follows, skip last chain. Purl across all sts.
Row 1 (RS): K7, pm, work row 1 of chart, pm, k7.
Row 2 (WS) and all WS rows: purl all sts, slipping m as you come to them.
Continue as established until row 101 has been worked, ending after a RS row. Carefully remove provisional CO and return live sts to second needle. Cut working yarn leaving a 24" tail. Thread tail onto tapestry needle and with wrong sides of fabric held together and RS facing, graft ends together using kitchener method. Adjust graft tension until it matches knitting tension; graft should be invisible and knitting should appear to be continuous. Do not cut kitchener tail. Weave in yarn from CO.

Finishing

Stretch knitting over bangle and sew long sides together using mattress stitch and tail from kitchener graft. Weave in any remaining ends so that they will be hidden on the interior side of bangle.

Finished Size

Cuff measures 1.75" wide, 9.5" circumference

Yarn

Cascade Heritage Silk (85% Superwash Merino Wool, 15% Mulberry Silk; 437 yd [400 m] 100 g): color 5633 Italian Plum, 1 hank.

Needles

Size 2 (2.75 mm) straight or double-pointed

Notions

162 (approx. 12 grams) size 6/0 brass colored beads, 1 flat-sided 1.75" wide, 2.75" diameter plastic bangle, fingering weight scrap yarn for provisional cast on, tapestry needle, scissors, size 1.25 mm crochet hook and 3 mm crochet hook.

Cuff shown used Beader's Paradise Czech glass beads in Brown Iris LT6E8 (beadersparadiseonline.com); China brand black lucite marbled bangle X000EXOSLV (amazon.com).

Gauge

34 stitches, 42 rows = 4" (10 cm) in stockinette stitch (unstretched)

Step 1: Following the feather chart for placement, knit to bead symbol and then load 1 bead onto hook, slip knit stitch off left needle and onto hook, then slide bead off hook and onto knit stitch. Return stitch to left knitting needle and knit as usual.

Step 2: Knitted bangle cover has been grafted using kitchener method, and tail is threaded onto tapestry needle for seaming.

Step 3: Stretch bangle cover around bangle and shift beaded pattern to the inside to make seaming easier. Working around the outside circumference of the bangle using mattress stitch, seam bangle cover closed. Weave in any remaining ends.

Step 4: Rotate bangle cover so that beaded pattern is now showing on the outside.

Knitting chart (B = bead; row numbers at right, stitch numbers at bottom):

Row	14	13	12	11	10	9	8	7	6	5	4	3	2	1
101									B	B				
99									B					
97								B						
95						B		B		B				
93						B		B		B				
91							B	B	B					
89					B			B			B			
87						B		B			B			
85							B	B	B					
83					B			B			B			
81						B		B			B			
79							B	B	B					
77					B			B			B			
75						B		B			B			
73							B	B	B					
71					B			B			B			
69						B		B			B			
67			B				B	B	B			B		
65				B				B				B		
63						B		B		B				
61							B	B	B					
59			B					B				B		
57				B				B			B			
55						B	B	B	B	B				
53			B					B				B		
51				B				B			B			
49						B		B		B				
47			B				B	B	B			B		
45				B				B			B			
43	B					B		B		B			B	
41		B					B	B	B			B		
39				B				B			B			
37	B					B		B		B			B	
35		B					B	B	B			B		
33				B				B			B			
31	B					B		B		B			B	
29		B					B	B	B			B		
27				B				B			B			
25						B		B		B				
23	B					B		B	B	B			B	
21		B						B			B			
19						B	B	B	B	B				
17								B						
15								B		B	B			
13	B							B	B					
11		B					B	B						
9				B	B		B	B	B					
7								B			B			
5								B						
3								B						
1								B						

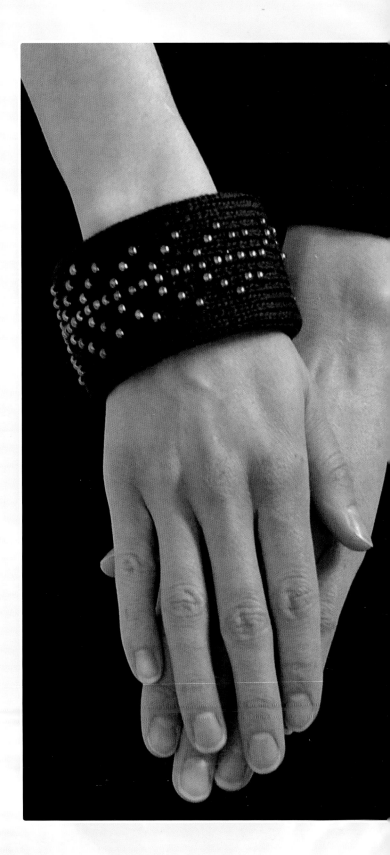

Lovebird Mittens

Cascade's Casablanca yarn perfectly captures the bright and cheerful shades of the lovebird! These sweet mittens were inspired by vintage Valentine's Day cards. Make a pair for yourself, and for all of your beloved friends!

Notes

- Make your mittens matching, or let the multi-colored yarn choose for you!
- Scrap yarn is an excellent stitch holder for thumb stitches as it is flexible and allows the wearer to try the mitten on as the knitting progresses.
- Thumb length may be adjusted by beginning decreases once the thumb knitting reaches the middle of the fingernail.

Glossary of abbreviations

beg – beginning
CC – contrast color
CO – cast on
inc – increase
k – knit
M1L – make one left increase: insert left hand needle under bar between stitches from front to back; knit through back loop.
M1R – make one right increase: insert left hand needle under bar between stitches from back to front; knit through front loop.

m – marker, markers
MC – main color
p – purl
rem – remaining
rep – repeat
pm – place marker
RS – right side
st st – stockinette stitch
st, sts – stitch, stitches
WS – wrong side

Finished Size

Designed to fit women's medium-sized hand (approx. 7–8" circumference, 7–75" long). Laid flat, mitten measures 4" wide, 9.75" long from cast on edge to top.

Yarn

Cascade 220 (100% Peruvian Highland Wool; 220 yd [200 m] 100 g) color: 9473 Gris (MC), 1 hank
Cascade Casablanca (60% wool, 25% silk, 15% mohair; 220 yd [200 m] 100 g): color 04 Poppy Field (CC), 1 hank. This is sufficient for two pairs of mittens.

Needles

Size 5 (6.75 mm) double-pointed

Notions

Scrap yarn, tapestry needle, scissors.

Gauge

26 stitches, 29 rounds = 4" (10 cm) in charted colorwork pattern

Left Mitten

Using MC and long-tail method, CO 52 sts. PM and join to beg knitting in the round in corrugated rib pattern.

Setup round: using MC, k2; using CC, k2 around all sts. Rep k2, k2 pattern alternating colors for one round.

Rounds 2–15: using MC, k2; using CC, p2 around all sts.

Change to st st and begin left hand knitting chart, working M1L inc for first st of thumb chart at beg of row 4 (note red reminder on chart). Continue following left hand knitting chart and thumb chart through round 20, then place 17 thumb sts on scrap yarn holder. Rejoin in the round and complete left hand knitting chart.

Cut yarns and thread MC onto tapestry needle, draw through rem 8 sts and fasten off.

To complete thumb, return held sts to double-pointed needles. Wind off CC until you reach the same color as thumb sts; cut wrong color yarn off ball and set aside.

Join CC and resume working thumb chart, beginning by picking up one st using CC in gap where thumb meets hand, following chart around the thumb, and ending by picking up one st in CC on other side of gap (19 sts).

Work thumb in the round until chart is complete and cut MC. K 1 round even, then begin decreasing:
Round 1: (k3, k2tog) 3 times, k4.
Round 2: (k2, k2tog) around.
Round 3: (k1, k2tog) around.
Round 4: k2tog around. Cut yarns, thread CC on to tapestry needle and draw through rem 4 sts. Weave in all ends on WS and block mittens to finished measurements.

Right Mitten

Work as above, using right hand knitting chart in place of left hand knitting chart.

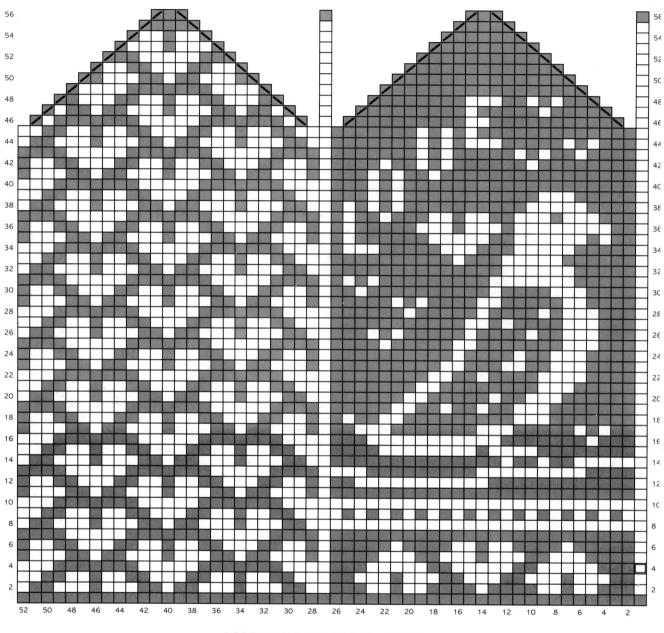

LEFT HAND KNITTING CHART

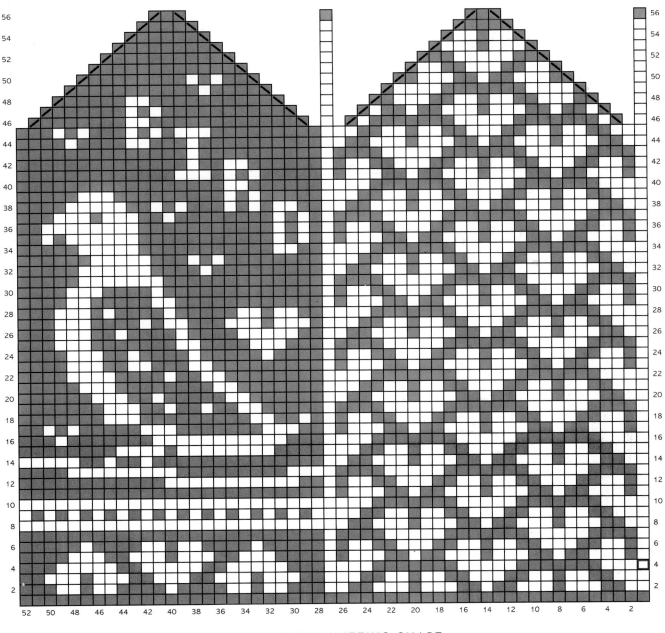

RIGHT HAND KNITTING CHART

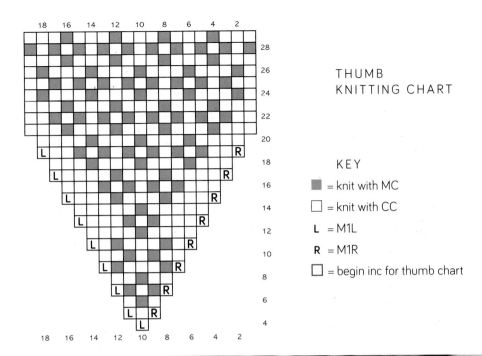

THUMB
KNITTING CHART

KEY

- ■ = knit with MC
- □ = knit with CC
- **L** = M1L
- **R** = M1R
- □ = begin inc for thumb chart

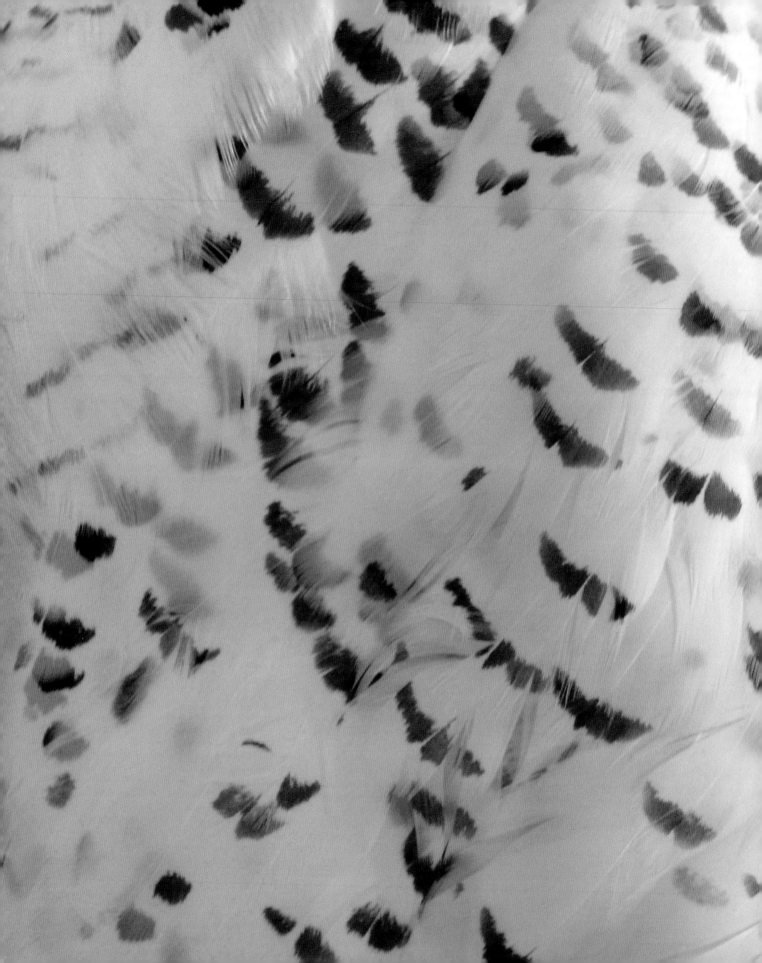

Shawls & Capelets

Snowy Owl Capelet

Murmuration Shawl

Feathered Shoulder Warmer

Wingtip Shawl

Snowy Owl Capelet

The beautiful camouflage patterning of the snowy owl is enlarged into abstract feather motifs in this elegant winter capelet. Knit in the round using steeks, this project is perfect for taking your colorwork knitting to the next level. Add a sweet satin ribbon to complete the look!

Notes

- When choosing a size, hold arms down at sides and measure around the fullest part of your bust and arms. Add 4–6" of ease depending upon personal fit preferences, considering what you may choose to wear underneath the capelet.
- Capelet is worked in the round using charted colorwork pattern and additional steek stitches. Once the knitting is completed, the steeks are reinforced by machine sewing or crocheting by hand and then cut apart.
- Satin ribbon is sewn along the neck edge by hand or machine.

Glossary of abbreviations

CC – contrast color
CO – cast on
dec – decrease, decreasing
k – knit
m – marker, markers
MC – main color

p – purl
rep – repeat
pm – place marker
RS – right side
sts – stitches
WS – wrong side

Finished Size

Small/Medium (28–38" bust):
17" deep, 46" bottom circumference
Large/X-Large (38–48" bust):
17" deep, 55" bottom circumference
Capelet shown is Small/Medium, modeled on 36" bust.

Yarn

Cascade 220 (100% Peruvian Highland Wool; 220 yd [200 m] 100g):
color 8555 Black (MC) 2 (2) hanks,
color 8505 White (CC) 2 (3) hanks.

Needles

Size 8 (5.0 mm) 16" and 40" circular

Notions

3 markers, 2 of one color and 1 of another color to mark beginning of round, tapestry needle, scissors, 3 yards of $^{7}/_{8}$" wide double-sided black satin ribbon, sewing needle, black sewing thread size H crochet hook, Sewing machine optional

Gauge

21 stitches, 26 rounds = 4" (10 cm) in stranded pattern

Capelet

Using longer circular needles and MC, CO 249 (297) sts. PM (odd color) and join to begin knitting in the round. K4 steek sts, pm, then work (k2, p2) ribbing around until 3 sts remain, pm, K3 steek sts. Continue as established working ribbing for body of capelet and keeping steek stitches in stockinette stitch until 10 rounds of ribbing are complete.

K1 round, dec 2 sts evenly. 247 (295) sts rem. Join CC and work first four steek sts as follows: k1 CC, k1 MC, k1 CC, k1 MC, sl m, work chart 1 10 (12) times around, sl m, k1 MC, k1 CC, k1 MC. Continue working steek

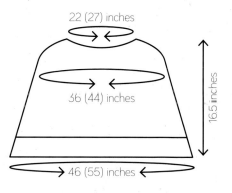

22 (27) inches

36 (44) inches

16.5 inches

46 (55) inches

sts in columns of alternating colors and complete chart 1.

Dec Round: Using CC, (K10, k2tog) around. 20(24) sts decreased, 227 (271) sts rem. Work rounds 1–20 of chart 2.

Dec Round: Using CC, (K9, k2tog) around. 20(24) sts decreased, 207 (247) sts rem. Work rounds 1–20 of chart 3.

Dec Round: Using CC, (K8, k2tog) around. 20 (24) sts decreased, 187 (223) sts rem.

Work rounds 1–29 of chart 4, changing to shorter circular needle when necessary and cutting MC after round 12 is completed. Remaining rounds and steek stitches will be worked in CC only. 50 (60) sts decreased, 137 (163) sts rem.

Bind off in CC and cut remaining yarn. Reinforce steek stitches on either side of center stitch using sewing machine or hand crochet method.

Cut straight up the middle between reinforcement lines until capelet is open along front.

Weave in remaining ends and tack down steek edges on WS of work using yarn needle and MC yarn that has been split in half lengthwise to reduce bulk.

Block to finished measurements, then sew satin ribbon along neck edge as follows: With RS facing, leave 1 yard hanging at right neck edge and pin top edge of ribbon along base of bind off stitches around full circumference of neckline, leaving a second long length of ribbon hanging at left neck edge. Stitch ribbon in place and unpin. Carefully fold ribbon up and over neckline and pin to WS of fabric. With RS still facing, stitch along the same sewing line as before, catching the ribbon in place on the WS. Remove pins and trim long ends to equal length for tying capelet at the neck.

STEEK REINFORCEMENT AND CUTTING

Step 1: Reinforcing with crochet: With RS of work facing using crochet hook and MC, work a column of single crochet stitches on either side of the center stitch beginning on the left at the ribbed hem. Use the left leg of the center stitch and the right leg of the stitch to the left. When you reach the bind off, finish off the column, rotate work, and work second column of crochet stitches from the neck down, this time using the remaining leg of the center stitch and the leg of the stitch immediately adjacent.

Step 2: When pulled carefully apart, the two lines of reinforcement reveal a column of strands in MC and CC to be cut. Take care not to cut the reinforcement yarn.

Step 3: Carefully begin cutting up the center between the two lines of reinforcement. Keep your hand or a firm piece of cardstock between the layers to prevent accidentally cutting through floats on the WS.

Step 4: Continue cutting up the entire length of the capelet until it can be opened flat.

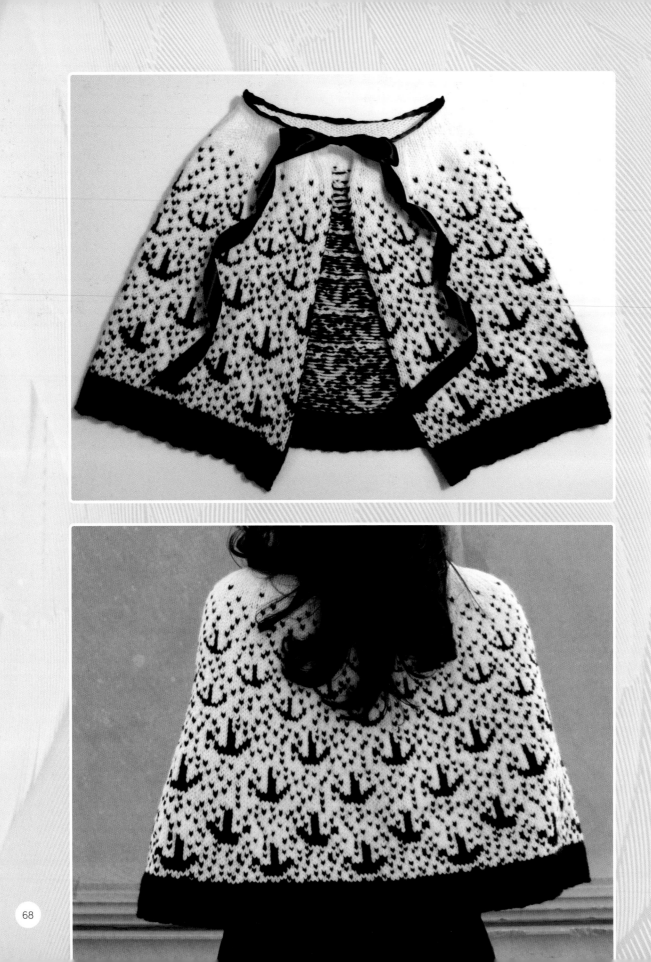

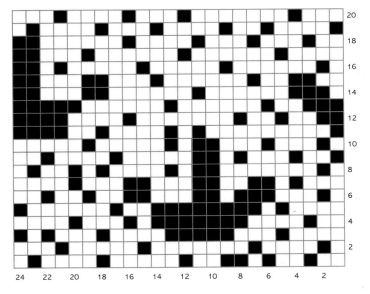

KNITTING CHART 1

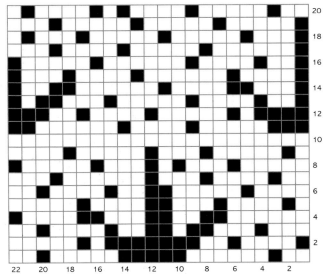

KNITTING CHART 2

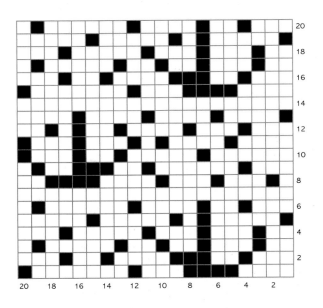

KNITTING CHART 3

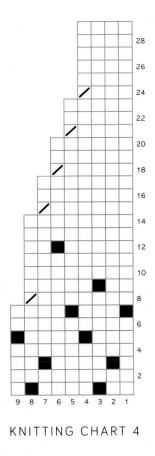

KNITTING CHART 4

KEY

 = k with MC

☐ = k with CC

╱ = k2tog

Murmuration Shawl

Graceful, waving birds border this sweet murmuration-inspired shawl. Lightweight yet warm, Heritage yarn is the perfect choice for between-season accessories. Combining a solid with the subtly variegated paints adds an additional layer of interest.

Notes

- Shawl is knitted from the bottom up, and will decrease by 4 sts every RS row.
- Use stitch markers to separate each chart repeat, and an odd-color marker to indicate the center of the shawl.
- When working stranded colorwork pattern, do not cut yarn when MC or CC goes unused for a few rows. Instead, leave unused color hanging at back of work and loosely carry up on the WS when it is to be used again. This will create a short vertical float on the back of the work.

Glossary of abbreviations

beg – begin, beginning
CC – contrast color
CO – cast on
dec – decrease, decreasing
k – knit
k2tog – knit two sts together
m – marker, markers
MC – main color
p – purl
rem – remain, remaining

rep – repeat
pm – place marker
RS – right side
sl m – slip marker
ssk – slip first st as if to knit, slip second st as if to knit, insert left hand needle through the front of both sts and knit them together.
sts – stitches
WS – wrong side

Stitch Guide

Rachis Ridges

Row 1 (WS): Knit.
Row 2 (RS): K2, sl m, ssk, k to 2 sts before m, k2tog, sl m, ssk, k to 2 sts before m, k2tog, sl m, k2.
Row 3 (WS): Purl.
Rows 4–16: Rep rows 2 and 3, ending after a RS row.

Shawl

Using MC and double-ended long-tail method, CO 492 sts. Do not join; shawl is worked back and forth in rows.

Beg on the WS and knit 1 row, placing markers as follows: k2, pm, k244, place center m, k244, pm, k2.

Work dec row as follows: k2, sl m, ssk, k to 2 sts before center m, k2tog, sl m, ssk, k to 2 sts before last m, k2tog, sl m, k2.

K 1 row, rep dec row, k 1 row (484 sts rem). RS is now facing; join CC and work charts through row 30 as follows: On RS, (work

Finished Size

Shawl measures 67.5" wide, 31" deep after blocking

Yarn

Cascade Heritage (75% Superwash Merino Wool; 437 yd [400 m] 100 g): color 5604 Denim (MC), 2 hanks.
Cascade Heritage Paints (75% Superwash Merino Wool; 437 yd [400 m] 100 g): color 9943 Ice Caves (CC), 1 hank.
Pattern uses nearly all of MC. Consider purchasing an additional "safety skein" if you are concerned about achieving correct gauge, or see note in pattern body about changing to CC sooner.

Needles

Size 4 (2.75 mm) 32" or longer circular; two size 4 (2.75 mm) double-pointed for 3-needle bind off

Notions

11 stitch markers (one odd-color marker for center), tapestry needle, scissors

Gauge

24 stitches, 35 rows = 4" (10 cm) in stockinette stitch after blocking

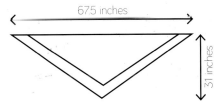

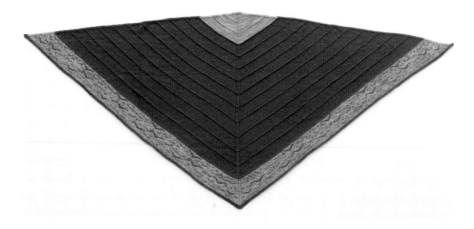

Right Edge Chart, work Body Chart 4 times, work Left Edge Chart) twice. On WS, (work Left Edge Chart, work Body Chart 4 times, work Right Edge Chart) twice. When charts are completed, 424 sts rem and RS is facing. Cut CC.

Using MC only, k2, sl m, ssk, k to 2 sts before center m, k2tog, sl m, ssk, k to 2 sts before last m, k2tog, sl m, k2.

With WS facing, beg Rachis Ridges pattern. Rep rows 1–16 10 times, then work row 1 once more (Note: consider working only 8–9 repeats and changing to CC sooner if MC is running low).

With RS facing, cut MC, join CC, and resume Rachis Ridges pattern on row 2.

Continue as established until 8 sts rem, ending after a WS row.

With RS facing, work final decrease row as follows: removing all m as you come to them, k2, ssk, k2tog, k2 (6 sts rem).

Arrange rem sts so that there are 3 each on two double-pointed needles and hold with RS of work together, WS facing.

Work 3-needle bind off, using circular needle tip for third needle.

Finishing

Soak, then pin shawl to finished measurements. Allow to dry completely and weave in all ends.

DOUBLE-ENDED LONG-TAIL CAST ON

Step 1: Grab two ends of your yarn, either from two different balls or the inside AND outside pull of your single skein. Tie them together (how doesn't really matter because you'll be taking this knot out, but I like a simple overhand knot). Drape the knot over your needle, one working end on either side.

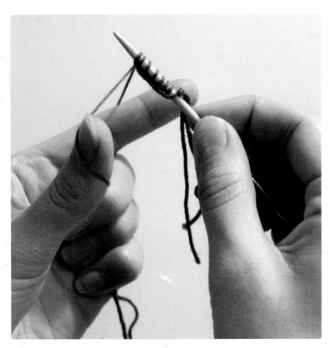

Step 2: Cast on using the long-tail method as usual, but don't count the knot as a stitch. Remember, you'll be taking it out!

Step 3: When cast on is complete, untie the beginning knot. Cut one of the working yarns leaving a 6" tail for weaving in. The remaining yarn will be used for your shawl.

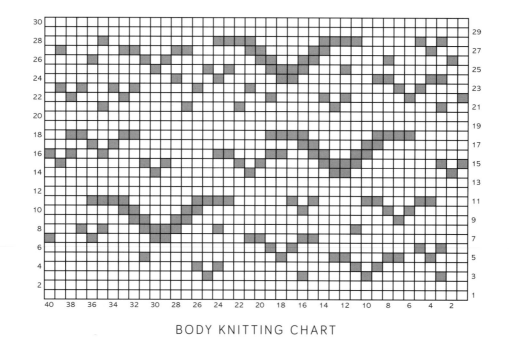

BODY KNITTING CHART

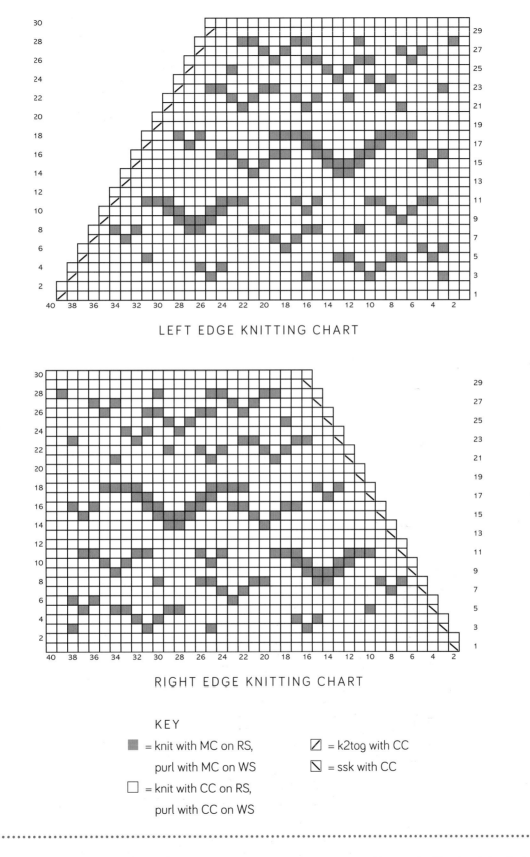

LEFT EDGE KNITTING CHART

RIGHT EDGE KNITTING CHART

KEY

■ = knit with MC on RS,
  purl with MC on WS

□ = knit with CC on RS,
  purl with CC on WS

◿ = k2tog with CC

◥ = ssk with CC

Feathered Shoulder Warmer

A quick and whimsical knit, the Feathered Shoulder Warmer doubles as a decorative garland. Make yours using the suggested yarns, or use leftovers from various projects to create a truly unique piece.

Glossary of abbreviations

BO – bind off
CO – cast on
k – knit
kfb – knit into the front and back of the stitch to increase
k2tog – knit two sts together
p – purl
rep – repeat
pm – place marker

RS – right side
sk2p – slip next stitch as if to knit, knit next two stitches together, then pass slipped stitch over.
ssk – slip first st as if to knit, slip second st as if to knit, insert left hand needle through the front of both sts and knit them together.
st, sts – stitch, stitches
WS – wrong side

Shoulder-warmer
Feathers

Small (Medium, Large): Make 8 small feathers in 220 Sport using size 6 needles (3 white, 3 black, 2 red), 8 medium feathers in 220 using size 8 needles, and 8 large feathers in Ecological Wool using size 10 needles. Leaving a 6" tail, CO 3 sts and work i-cord for 1.5". Turn work and beg working back and forth in rows:

Row 1: (WS) K1, p1, k1.
Row 2: (RS) Kfb, kfb, k1.
Row 3 and all WS rows through feather tip shaping: K2, p to last 2 sts, k2.
Row 4: K1, kfb, kfb, k2.
Row 6: K2, kfb, kfb, k3.
Row 8: K3, kfb, kfb, k4.
Row 10: K2, ssk, kfb, kfb, k1, k2tog, k2.

Rep rows 9 and 10 until work measures 6 (7, 8)" from row 1, ending on a RS row. Shape feather tip:
Rows 1, 3, 5, 7 (WS): K2, p to last 2 sts, k2.
Row 2 (RS): K2, ssk, k3, k2tog, k2.
Row 4: Knit.
Row 6: K2, ssk, k1, k2tog, k2.
Row 8: K2, sk2p, k2.
Row 9: Knit.
Row 10: Ssk, k1, k2tog.
Row 11: Slip first st as if to k, BO all sts.
I-cord: Using 220 and size 8 needles, work 4 stitch i-cord for 60" or desired length. BO and weave in ends. Using 6" tails from feather CO, sew feathers in random order to center 36" of i-cord. Weave in remaining ends. Block as desired.

Finished Size

I-cord measures approximately 60" long; longest feather measures 10".

Yarn

Cascade Ecological Wool (100% Peruvian Highland Wool; 478 yd [437 m] 250 g): color 8015 Natural, 1 hank.
Cascade 220 (100% Peruvian Highland Wool; 220 yd [200 m] 100 g): color 9473 Gris, 1 hank.
Cascade 220 Sport (100% Peruvian Highland Wool; 164 yd [150 m] 50 g): color 8505 White, 1 hank; color 8555 Black, 1 hank; color 8995 Christmas Red, 1 hank.

Needles

Size 10 (6 mm) double-pointed, size 8 (5 mm) double-pointed, size 6 (4.25 mm) double-pointed

Notions

Tapestry needle, scissors

Gauge

Not critical for this project; various yarns and needle sizes will result in multiple gauges. See finished size information for feather measurements.

Step 1: Cast on the number of stitches called for in the pattern using your preferred method.

Step 2: Slide work to other end of needle to begin. Note that the yarn is coming off the last stitch, not the first one near the needle tip.

Step 3: Knit across all stitches.

Step 4: Slide work to other end of needle. Repeat steps 3 and 4 until i-cord is desired length; it will take approximately 5 rows before your stitches will begin to curve together to form the cord. Stick with it!

Wingtip Shawl

The wingspan of the Osprey boasts an array of blacks, grays, and palest white, all inspiration for the Wingtip Shawl. This water-loving bird is unusually omnipresent: it is the only known species of bird that lives worldwide, and has been written about for centuries throughout various cultures. Take comfort in this cozy shawl, perfect for keeping your shoulders warm on your own adventures!

Notes

- Shawl is knitted in two halves, then grafted together using kitchener stitch.

Shawl
Left Half

Using CC1 and long-tail method, CO 16 sts. Do not join.

Row 1 (WS): Knit.

Row 2 (RS): Kfb, k to end.

Row 3: Knit.

Rows 4, 6, 8, 10: As for row 2.

Rows 5, 7, 9: K1, p until 2 sts rem, k2.

Row 11: K1, p until 11 sts rem, k11.

Row 12: As for row 2.

Row 13: K1, p until 12 sts rem, k12.

Row 14: BO 10 sts, k to end.

*Row 15: K1, p until 2 sts rem, K2, CO 10 sts using reverse loop or other preferred method.

Rows 16, 18, 20, 22, 24, 26: Kfb, k to end.

Row 17: K1, p until 13 sts rem, k13.

Row 19: K1, p until 14 sts rem, k14.

Row 21, 23, 25: K1, p until 2 sts rem, k2.

Row 27: K1, p until 11 sts rem, k11.

Row 28: Kfb, k to end.

Row 29: K1, p until 12 sts rem, k12.

Row 30: BO 10 sts.* Cut CC1; join CC2 and k to end.

Using CC2, rep from * to * twice. Cut CC2; join CC3 and knit to end.

Using CC3, rep from * to * twice. Cut CC3; join CC4 and knit to end.

Using CC4, rep from * to * twice. Cut CC4; join MC and knit to end.

Using MC, rep from * to * five times, then from * through Row 26 once more.

Place sts on holder or scrap yarn and set aside to work Right half.

Right half

Using CC1 and long-tail method, CO 16 sts. Do not join.

Row 1 (WS): Knit.

Row 2 (RS): K until 2 sts rem, kfb, k1.

Row 3: Knit.

Rows 4, 6, 8, 10: As for row 2.

Rows 5, 7, 9, 11: K2, p until 1 st rem, k1.

Row 12: As for row 2.

Row 13: K11, p until 1 st rem, K1.

Row 14: As for row 2.

Row 15: BO 10, k1, p until 1 st rem, K1.

*Row 16: K to end, CO 10 sts using reverse loop or other preferred method.

Row 17: K12, p until 1 st rem, k1.

Row 18, 20, 22, 24, 26, 28: K until 2 sts rem, kfb, k1.

Row 19: K13, p to last st, k1.

Row 21, 23, 25, 27: K2, p until 1 st rem, k1.

Row 29: K11, p until 1 st rem, k1.

Row 30: K until 2 sts rem, kfb, k1.

Row 31: BO 10 sts. *Cut CC1; join CC2 and p until 1 st rem, k1.

Finished Size

Shawl measures 58" wide, 20" deep after blocking

Yarn

Cascade 220 Sport (100% Peruvian Highland Wool; 164 yd [150 m] 50 g): color 8505 White (MC), 4 hanks; color 8555 Black (CC1), 1 hank; color 4002 Jet (CC2), 1 hank; color 8400 Charcoal Grey (CC3), 1 hank; color 8401 Silver Grey (CC4), 1 hank.

Needles

Size 6 (4.25 mm) 24" circular

Notions

Tapestry needle, scissors.

Gauge

22 stitches, 32 rows = 4" (10 cm) in stockinette stitch

Glossary of abbreviations

BO – bind off

CC – contrast color

CO – cast on

k – knit

kfb – knit in the front and back of stitch; increase made

m – marker, markers

MC – main color

p – purl

rem – remain, remaining

rep – repeat

RS – right side

sts – stitches

WS – wrong side

Using CC2, rep from * to * twice. Cut CC2; join CC3 and knit to end.

Using CC3, rep from * to * twice. Cut CC3; join CC4 and knit to end.

Using CC4, rep from * to * twice. Cut CC4; join MC and knit to end.

Using MC, rep from * to * five times, then from * through Row 28 once more.

Return held sts from left half to needle

and hold shawl pieces with WS together, RS facing out.

Finishing

Graft live sts together using kitchener method. Adjust graft tension to match knitting tension. Weave in all ends and block to finished measurements.

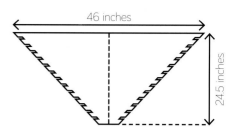

REVERSE LOOP CAST ON

Step 1: With correct side facing (see pattern instructions), tension yarn around left index finger by holding finger on top of working yarn,

Step 2: then tilting wrist down to point at self,

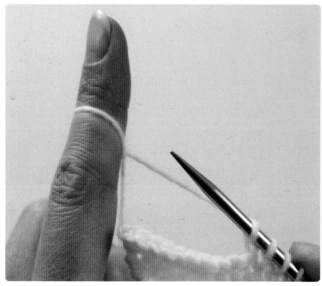

Step 3: then rolling wrist away.

Step 4: Slide new stitch onto right hand needle. Repeat for a total of 10 new stitches.

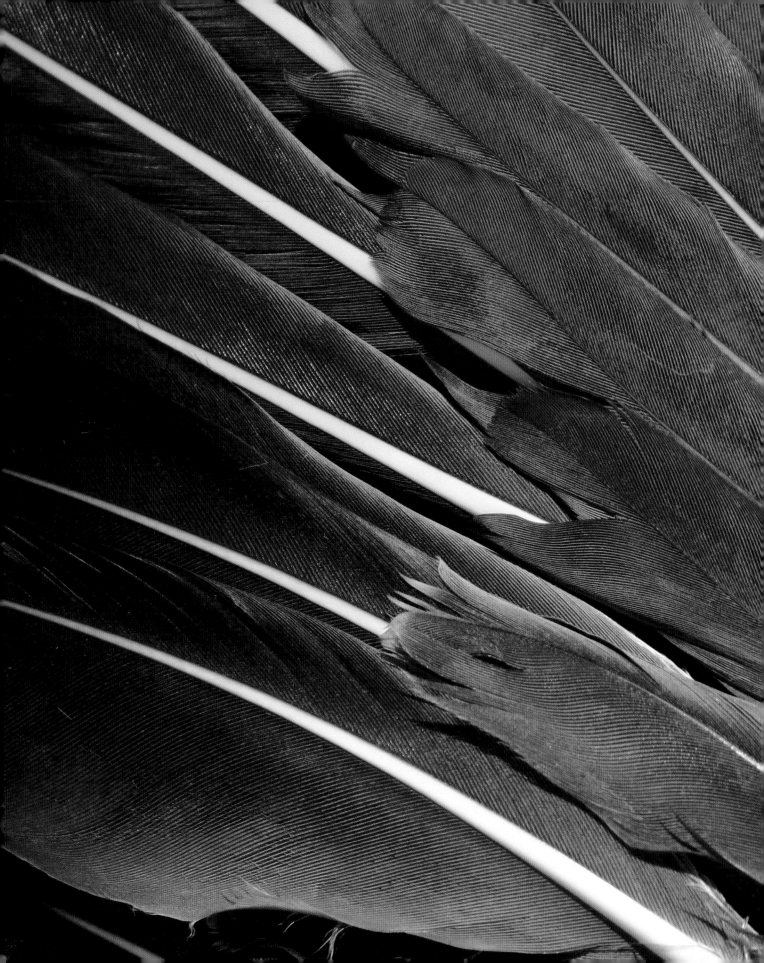

Sweaters

Starling Cardigan

Bright pinpricks of color echo the feathers of the Starling songbird. Cozy superwash wool and comfortable three-quarter length sleeves make this cropped cardigan a staple of any wardrobe!

Notes

- Cardigan is worked top-down in stockinette stitch, with body worked back and forth in rows and sleeves worked in the round.
- Button bands are picked up and knitted after body is completed.
- Optional patch pockets are knit separately and sewn to finished sweater.

Glossary of abbreviations

BO – bind off
CC – contrast color
CO – cast on
dec – decrease, decreasing
k – knit
k2tog – knit next two sts together; decrease made
kfb – knit in the front and back of next stitch; increase made
m – marker, markers
MC – main color
p – purl

pm – place marker
rep – repeat
RS – right side
sm – slip marker
ssk – slip first stitch as if to knit, slip next stitch as if to knit, insert left hand needle through the fronts of both slipped sts and knit together; decrease made
st st – stockinette stitch
sts – stitches
WS – wrong side

Cardigan

Using MC and larger circular needles, CO 48 (50, 52, 56, 62) sts as follows: CO 2 (2, 2, 2, 4) sts, pm, CO 5 (5, 5, 5, 6) sts, pm, CO 34 (36, 38, 40, 44) sts, pm, CO 5 (5, 5, 5, 6) sts, pm, CO 2 (2, 2, 2, 4) sts. Do not join.

Row 1 (RS): K1, (kfb, sm, kfb, knit to 1 st before m) 3 times, kfb, sm, kfb, k1.

Row 2 and all WS rows: Purl all sts.

Row 3: Kfb, (k to 1 st before m, kfb, sm, kfb) 4 times, k to last st, kfb.

Row 5: (K to 1 st before m, kfb, sm, kfb) 4 times, k to end.

Rep rows 2–5 11 (12, 13, 14, 15) times more; 84 (90, 96, 102, 110) sts between back markers.

Divide for sleeves: k to first m, remove m, transfer 55 (59, 63, 67, 72) sleeve sts to yarn holder, remove m, k to next m, remove m, transfer 55 (59, 63, 67, 72) sleeve sts to yarn holder, remove m, k to end. 162 (174, 186, 198, 216) body sts rem on needles.

Continue working back and forth in st st on body sts until sweater measures 11 (11.5, 12, 12, 13)" from divide for sleeves, ending after a RS row.

Cut MC and using smaller circular needle, join CC and purl across all sts, dec 2 (2, 2, 2, 0) sts evenly.

Ribbing setup row: K3, p2, (k2, p2) until 3 sts rem, k3.

Finished Size

32.5 (35, 37, 40, 43.5)" bust. Modeled in size 35 with 1" of positive ease.

Yarn

Cascade 220 Superwash Quatros (100% Superwash Wool; 220 yd [200 m] 100 g): color 1957 Antigua (MC), 3 (4, 4, 4, 5) hanks
Cascade 220 Superwash (100% Superwash Wool; 220 yd (200m)/100g): color 854 Navy (CC), 1 (1, 2, 2, 2) hanks.

Needles

Size 7 (4.5 mm) 29" circular and double-pointed; size 5 (3.75 mm) 40" circular and double-pointed.

Notions

Five ¾" buttons, four stitch markers, scrap yarn or stitch holders, tapestry needle, scissors.

Cardigan shown used Dill Buttons style number 330718, color 20 (dill-buttons.com).

Gauge

20 stitches, 26 rounds = 4" (10 cm) in stockinette stitch using larger needles

Row 2: P3, k2, (p2, k2) until 3 sts rem, p3.
Rep rows 2 and 3 until ribbing measures 2".
BO in pattern.

Sleeves

With RS facing, transfer held sts to larger double-pointed needles, pm and join MC to begin working in the round.
K 7 rounds even.
Dec round: K1, k2tog, k until 3 sts rem, ssk, k1.
Rep last 8 rounds 8 (8, 9, 9, 9) times more, 37 (41, 43, 47, 52) sts rem.
K 5 rounds even.
Cut MC and using smaller double-pointed needles, join CC and knit one round even.
For sizes 32 and 35 only: Ribbing setup row: K1, k2tog, p2, (k2, p2) around.
For sizes 37 and 40 only: Ribbing setup row: K1, kfb, p1, (k2, p2) around.
All sizes: Work in k2, p2 rib for 2".
BO in pattern.
Repeat for second sleeve.

Button bands

With RS facing, using smaller circular needles and CC, begin at the bottom of the right front and pick up 274 (286, 302, 314, 330) sts as follows: 76 (78, 82, 84, 88) sts between right front hem and beg of neckline shaping, 122 (130, 138, 146, 154) sts along right neckline, back neck, and left neckline, 76 (78, 82, 84, 88) sts between end of neckline shaping and left front hem. Do not join.
Row 2 (WS): P2, (k2, p2) to end.
Row 3: K2, (p2, k2) to end.
Rows 4–6: Rep rows 2 and 3.
Row 7: K2, BO next 3 sts (note that first two sts are not part of the BO), (work next 13 [14, 15, 15, 16] sts in rib pattern as established, BO next three sts) four times, work in rib pattern as established to end of row.
Row 8: Work in rib pattern as established until first BO gap is reached. Turn work to RS and using cable method, CO 3 sts. Turn work to WS and continue in rib as established,
repeating turn and cast on for each button hole bind off space.
Row 9: Resume working in rib pattern across all sts.
Rows 10–13: Rep rows 2 and 3.
Row 14: BO all sts in rib pattern.

Pockets (make two)

Using smaller needles and CC, CO 20 sts.
Row 1 (RS): K3, (p2, k2) across until 3 sts rem, k3.
Row 2: P3, (k2, p2) across until 3 sts rem, p3.
Rep rows 1 and 2 until ribbing measures 1".
Continue in stockinette stitch (knit on RS, purl on WS) for 2" more. Pocket measures 3" long. BO all sts leaving a long tail to sew pockets onto sweater fronts using mattress stitch, leaving top open for use.

Finishing

Weave in ends and block to finished measurements. Sew buttons onto left band across from buttonholes.

PICKING UP STITCHES FOR BUTTON BANDS

Step 1: With RS facing, insert right hand needle tip into space between the selvedge stitch and first full stitch from front to back.

Step 2: Wrap yarn around needle as if to knit.

Step 3: Pull new stitch through fabric to RS. Continue in this manner, picking up approximately 4 stitches for every 5 rows of knitting.

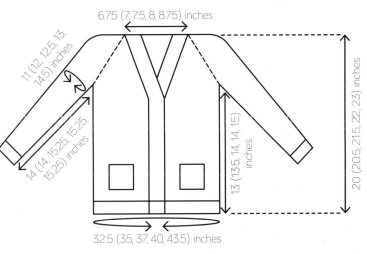

6.75 (7, 7.5, 8, 8.75) inches

11 (12, 12.5, 13, 14.5) inches

14 (14, 15.25, 15.25, 15.25) inches

13 (13.5, 14, 14, 15) inches

20 (20.5, 21.5, 22, 23) inches

32.5 (35, 37, 40, 43.5) inches

Raven Pullover

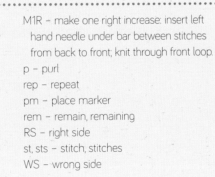

Black as night with sleek ribbing and a hint of folded wings, the Raven Pullover is as dramatic as it is practical. Hard-wearing Greenland creates a flexible fabric with fantastic stitch definition that can be machine washed and dried.

Notes

- Body is worked in the round from the bottom up, then divided to work front and back separately.
- Sleeves are worked in the round from cuff to shoulder, then sewn into armholes.
- Raven Chart includes RS rows only; on WS rows, work sts as they appear (i.e. knit the knits and purl the purls).

Glossary of abbreviations

beg – begin, beginning
BO – bind off
CO – cast on
dec – decrease, decreasing
k – knit
k2tog – knit two sts together
m – marker, markers
M1L – make one left increase: insert left hand needle under bar between stitches from front to back; knit through back loop.

M1R – make one right increase: insert left hand needle under bar between stitches from back to front; knit through front loop.
p – purl
rep – repeat
pm – place marker
rem – remain, remaining
RS – right side
st, sts – stitch, stitches
WS – wrong side

Finished Size

40 (44, 48, 52, 56)" chest circumference, intended to be worn with 4–6" positive ease. Modeled in size 44 with 6" of positive ease.

Yarn

Cascade Greenland (100% Superwash Merino; 137 yd [125 m] 100 g): color 3503 Black, 10 (11, 13, 14, 15) skeins.

Needles

Size 8 (5.0 mm) 32" circular, 16" circular and double-pointed

Notions

Stitch holders or scrap yarn, two stitch markers, tapestry needle, scissors

Gauge

18 stitches, 26 rows = 4" (10 cm) in stockinette stitch
20 stitches, 26 rows = 4" (10 cm) in k2, p2 rib (slightly stretched)

Stitch Patterns

K2, P2 rib worked in the round:
Round 1 and all subsequent rounds: *K 2, p 2; rep from * around all sts.
K2, P2 rib worked flat (in rows):
Row 1: *K2, p2; rep from * across all sts.
Row 2: Work sts as they appear (knit the knits and purl the purls).
Rep row 1 and 2 for pattern.

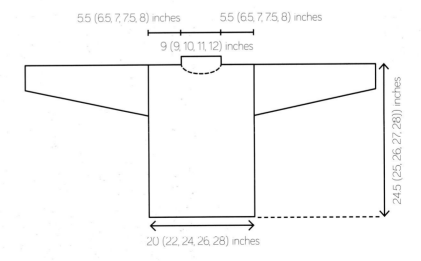

5.5 (6.5, 7, 7.5, 8) inches   5.5 (6.5, 7, 7.5, 8) inches

9 (9, 10, 11, 12) inches

24.5 (25, 26, 27, 28)) inches

20 (22, 24, 26, 28) inches

Pullover
Sweater Body
Using longer circular needle and long-tail method, CO 200 (220, 240, 260, 280) sts. PM and join to beg knitting in the round in k2, p2 rib.

Work in rib until body measures 15.5 (15.5, 16, 17, 17.5)" from beg.

Divide to work front and back separately, beginning with the front: BO 2 (2, 4, 4, 6) sts, work in rib pattern on next 98 (108, 116, 126, 134) sts, place rem 100 (110, 120, 130, 140) sts on a holder or scrap yarn.

Turn and beg working back and forth in k2, p2 rib until work measures 7 (7.5, 8, 8, 8.5)" from divide, ending on a WS row.

Shape front neck (RS): work 34 (38, 41, 44, 47) sts in rib pattern, place rem 64 (70, 75, 82, 87) sts on second holder.

Decrease row: Turn work and p2tog, rib to end.

Next row: Work in rib as established.

Rep last two rows 5 times more; 6 sts dec, 28 (32, 35, 38, 41) sts rem.

Place rem sts on a holder.

Return to 64 (70, 75, 82, 87) held sts (on second holder) and with RS facing, leave center 30 (32, 34, 38, 40) sts on holder for front neck and return 34 (38, 41, 44, 47) sts for right shoulder to needles.

With RS still facing, rejoin yarn and work decrease row as follows: ssk, rib to end.

Next row: work in rib as established.

Rep last two rows 5 times more; 6 sts dec, 28 (32, 35, 38, 41) sts rem.

Place rem sts on a holder.

Back
With RS facing, return 100 (110, 120, 130, 140) held sts to longer circular needles and rejoin yarn.

BO 2 (2, 4, 4, 6) sts, work in rib as established on rem 98 (108, 116, 126, 134) sts.

Turn and work a WS row in k2, p2 rib.

Next row (RS): work 8 (13, 17, 22, 26) sts in rib pattern as established, pm, work Raven Chart over center 82 sts, pm, work rem 8 (13, 17, 22, 26) sts in rib pattern as established.

Next Row (WS): work sts as they appear; knit the knits and purl the purls.

Rep last two rows until Raven Chart is

completed, working pattern on RS rows and all sts as they appear on WS rows.

Work even in rib pattern as established until back measures 9 (9.5, 10, 10, 10.5)" from divide, ending on a WS row.

Place first 28 (32, 35, 38, 41) sts on a holder for right shoulder, place center 42 (44, 46, 50, 52) sts on another holder for back neck, then place rem 28 (32, 35, 38, 41) sts on a holder for left shoulder.

Sleeves (make two)

Using double-pointed needles and long-tail method, CO 52 (56, 60, 60, 64) sts. PM and join to beg knitting in the round in k2, p2 rib.

Work in rib until sleeve measures 3" from beg.

Work increase round: K1, M1L, work in rib as established until 2 sts rem, M1R, k1.

Rep increase round every 7th round 9 times more, then every 11th round 4 times, incorporating increase sts into rib pattern: 80 (84, 88, 88, 92) sts.

Work even until sleeve measures 21 (22, 22.5, 22.5, 23)" from beg.

BO all sts in pattern.

Finishing

Beginning with the left shoulder, return 28 (32, 35, 38, 41) held sts from front left shoulder to double-pointed or circular needles and 28 (32, 35, 38, 41) held sts from back left shoulder to needles.

With RS held together and WS facing, work 3-needle bind off to complete left shoulder. Repeat for right shoulder.

Neckband: With RS facing and using shorter circular needles, join yarn at back left neck and pick up 12 sts down front left neck shaping, work in rib pattern as established across held front neck sts, pick up 12 sts up front right neck shaping, work in rib pattern as established across held back neck sts: 96 (100, 104, 112, 116) sts.

PM and join in the round to continue working neckband in rib pattern for 2".

BO all sts in pattern.

Sew sleeves into armholes.

Weave in all ends on WS and block to finished measurements.

MAKE ONE LEFT AND RIGHT INCREASES

Step 1: Make one left: insert left hand needle under bar between stitches from front to back; knit through back loop of stitch to twist it closed.

Step 2: Make one right: insert left hand needle under bar between stitches from back to front; knit through front loop of stitch to twist it closed.

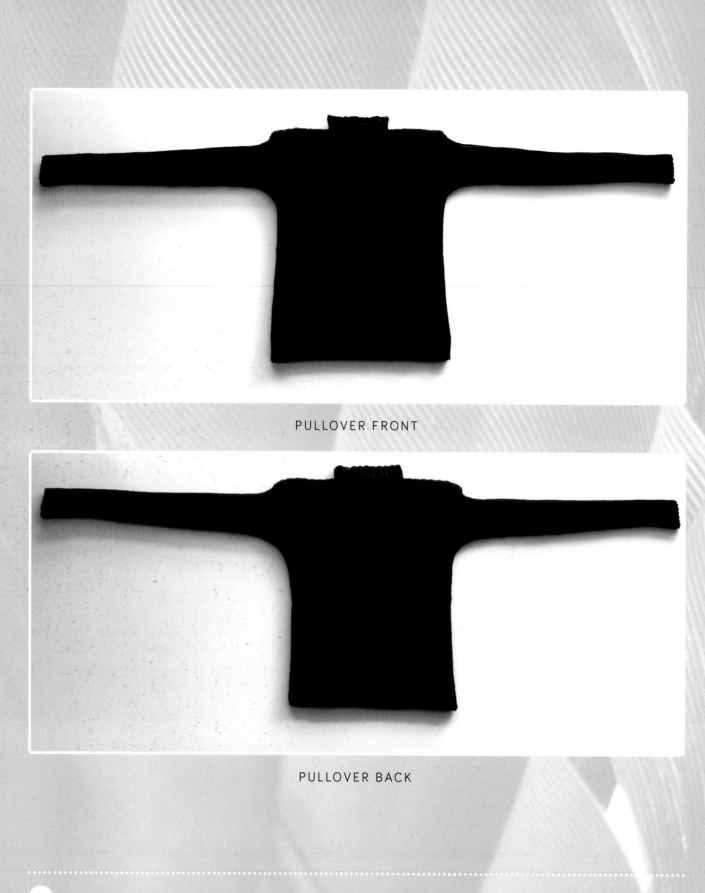

PULLOVER FRONT

PULLOVER BACK

KNITTING CHART

KEY

☐ = k on RS   ⊟ = p   ◳ = ssk

◿ = k2tog   ◲ = pfb   ■ = no stitch

Contour Feathers Pullover

Classic pinprick patterning with a modern twist! Subtle stranded colorwork hints at feathers and birds flying in the distance, bordered by rustic garter stitch. Cozy and warm, the Contour Feathers pullover is perfect for layering on a crisp winter day.

Notes

- Do not cut yarn when MC or CC goes unused for a few rounds. Instead, leave unused color hanging at back of work and loosely carry up on the WS when it is to be used again. This will create a short vertical float on the back of the work.
- Strand MC over and CC under in feather panels, but reverse this for the pinprick pattern to avoid distorted, elongated stitches.

Glossary of abbreviations

beg – begin
BO – bind off
CC – contrast color
CO – cast on
dec – decrease, decreasing
dpns – double-pointed needles
k – knit
m – marker, markers
M1L – make one left increase: insert left hand needle under bar between stitches from front to back; knit through back loop.

M1R – make one right increase: insert left hand needle under bar between stitches from back to front; knit through front loop.
MC – main color
p – purl
patt – pattern
pm – place marker
rem – remains, remaining
rep – repeat
RS – right side
st, sts – stitch, stitches
WS – wrong side

Stitch Patterns
Garter Stitch (worked in the round)
Round 1 (RS): Purl.
Round 2 (RS): Knit.
Rep round 1 and 2.

Pinprick Pattern
See Pinprick Chart

Pullover
Sleeves (make two)
Using CC, smaller dpns, and long tail method, CO 40 sts. PM and join to beg knitting in the round. Work in garter st for 6 rounds, beg with a purl round.

Change to larger dpns, join MC and work Sleeve Chart for 32 rounds.

Change to smaller dpns and knit two rounds in CC, then beg Pinprick pattern. AT THE SAME TIME, inc two sts every 14th (7th, 5th, 4th, 4th) round 3 (6, 8, 10, 12) times as follows: k1 st in pattern, using MC M1L, work around in patt until 1 st rem before m, using MC M1R, k1. Always work inc in MC, then incorporate new sts into Pinprick pattern on subsequent rounds. 46 (52, 56, 60, 64) sts.

Finished Size

32 (36, 40, 44, 48)" bust circumference; sample garment is 36" bust modeled with .5" positive ease. Choose the larger size if you are between measurements.

Yarn

Cascade Ecological Wool (100% Peruvian Highland Wool; 478 yd [437 m] 250 g): Color 8015 Natural (MC), 2 (2, 2, 2, 3) hanks, Color 8049 Tarnish (CC), 1 (1, 1, 1, 1) hank.

Needles

Set of 5 size 9 (5.5 mm) double-pointed, 16" circular, and 32" circular; set of 5 size 10 (6.0 mm) double-pointed and 32" circular

Notions

4 stitch markers (3 of one color, 1 different to mark beg of round), stitch holders or scrap yarn, tapestry needle, scissors

Gauge

16 stitches, 22 rounds = 4" (10 cm) in pinprick pattern on smaller needles after blocking.

Work even in patt until sleeve measures 17 (17, 17, 18, 18)" from CO edge, ending after pattern round 3 or 6. Cut yarns and place sts on a holder or set needles aside until body is ready for joining.

Body

Using CC, smaller circular needles, and long-tail method, CO 128 (144, 160, 176, 192) sts. PM and join to beg knitting in the round. Work in garter st for 6 rounds, beg with a purl round.

Change to larger circular needles, join MC and work Body Chart for 32 rounds.

Change to smaller circular needles and knit two rounds in CC, then begin Pinprick pattern. Work even in Pinprick pattern until body measures 16 (16.5, 16.5, 17, 17)" from CO edge, ending after pattern round 3 or 6.

Join sleeves to body as follows: using MC and smaller circular needles, k 62 (70, 78, 86, 94) body sts, pm, place next 4 body sts on a holder, place first 2 sleeve sts from first sleeve on a holder, k around 42 (48, 52, 56, 60) sts from same sleeve, place last 2 sleeve sts from same sleeve on a holder, pm, k next 60 (68, 76, 84, 92) body sts, pm, place first 2 sleeve sts from second sleeve on a holder, k around 42 (48, 52, 56, 60) sts from same sleeve, place last 2 sleeve sts from same sleeve on a holder, place beg of round m, place next 4 sts of body on a holder (two unworked sts and two sts from beg of joining round).

Resume working in Pinprick pattern, reading your knitting to determine placement of CC stitches as needed on sleeve and body sts, and AT THE SAME TIME begin raglan shaping, keeping decreases and the 2 knit sts between decreases in MC throughout as follows:

Using MC k1, k2tog, (work in Pinprick pattern to 3 sts before next m, using MC ssk, k1, sl m, k1, k2tog) three times, work in Pinprick patt to 3 sts before last m, using MC ssk, k1. Work 1 round even.

Continuing as established, alternate raglan shaping rounds and even rounds until 72 (72, 76, 84, 84) sts rem, changing to shorter circular needles when needed. If last round worked was not in MC only, work 1 round even in MC.

SEAMLESS NECKLINE FINISHING

Step 1: With RS of work facing, roll the edge of the neckline towards you until you can clearly see the V-shaped bound off stitches.

Step 2: Thread yarn tail onto tapestry needle. Skip first V-shaped stitch of bound off edge and insert needle under both legs of the following stitch from front to back.

Shape back neck: using MC, k to 1 st before first m, sl next st as if to purl, bring yarn to front of work, return st to left needle and bring yarn to back of work. One stitch has been wrapped. Turn to WS and purl back to beg of round. Cut MC and resume knitting in the round with CC only: K 1 round, working wrap when you come to it by inserting right hand needle into wrap first, then into stitch to be worked and working wrap and stitch together. Purl 1 round, knit 1 round, purl 1 round, knit 1 round. BO all sts in purl.

Finishing

Graft underarm sts together, attaching 4 sleeve sts to 4 body sts using kitchener method.

Weave in all ends following finishing photos for seamless neckline. Soak sweater and block to finished measurements.

Step 3: Loosely draw yarn through, then insert needle into the heart of the last bound off stitch, where the tail originated.

Step 4: Gently tighten yarn, adjusting tension until the size of the "stitch" just made matches the other bound off stitches. It should seamlessly bridge the gap between the first and last bound off stitches. Weave in end on WS of work.

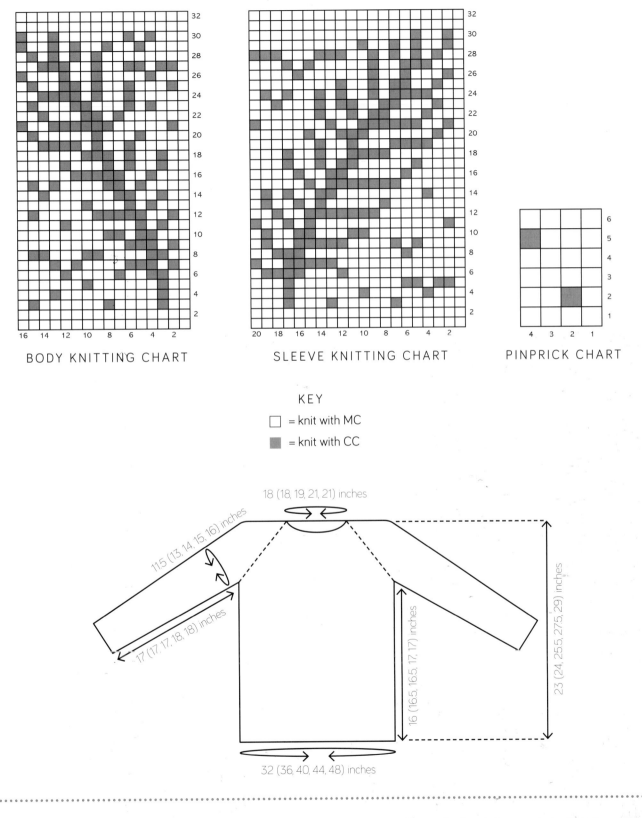

BODY KNITTING CHART

SLEEVE KNITTING CHART

PINPRICK CHART

KEY

☐ = knit with MC

■ = knit with CC

18 (18, 19, 21, 21) inches

11.5 (13, 14, 15, 16) inches

17 (17, 17, 18, 18) inches

16 (16.5, 16.5, 17, 17) inches

23 (24, 25.5, 27.5, 29) inches

32 (36, 40, 44, 48) inches

Bluebird on My Shoulder Cardigan

Bluebirds are synonymous with happiness and cheer. From Louis Armstrong to Cinderella, the bluebird appears throughout popular culture as a symbol of sweetness and delight. Wearing this cardigan you'll find one on your shoulder, and may joy follow you!

Notes

- Sweater is worked in pieces and assembled using mattress stitch. Consider leaving long tails at the cast on edge of each piece to use for seaming.
- Bluebird Chart is worked using intarsia for larger motifs, with embroidery details added after knitting is completed.

Glossary of abbreviations

beg – begin, beginning

BO – bind off

CC – contrast color

CO – cast on

dec – decrease, decreasing

inc – increase

k – knit

M1L – make one left increase: insert left hand needle under bar between stitches from front to back; knit through back loop.

M1R – make one right increase: insert left hand needle under bar between stitches from back to front; knit through front loop.

M1LP – make one left purl increase: insert left hand needle under bar between stitches from front to back; purl through back loop.

M1RP – make one right purl increase: insert left hand needle under bar between stitches from back to front; purl through front loop.

MC – main color

p – purl

pm – place marker

rep – repeat

RS – right side

st st – stockinette stitch

sts – stitches

WS – wrong side

Cardigan
Sleeves (make two)

Using smaller straight needles and MC, CO 54 (58, 62, 66, 70) sts. Work in k2, p2 ribbing until cuff measures 2", ending on a WS row. Change to larger needles and work 2 rows in st st. Join CC1 and work 2 rows in st st. Cut CC1 and resume using MC, working 5 more rows in st st. Increase row (WS): p1, M1LP, p until 1 st rem, M1RP, p1.

Continue working even in st st, rep inc row every 10th row 1 time, then every 11th row 8 times. Note: right side increase rows are worked as follows: k1, M1R, k until 1 st rem, M1L, k1. 74 (78, 82, 86, 90) sts. Work even until sleeve measures 17 (17, 17.5,

Finished Size

34 (36.5, 39, 41.5, 44)" bust circumference. Modeled in size 34 with 1" negative ease.

Yarn

Cascade 220 Superwash Sport (100% Superwash Merino Wool; 137 yd [125 m] 50 g): color 817 Aran (MC), 10 (10, 11, 12, 13) hanks;
Color 845 Denim (CC1), 1 hank
Color 818 Mocha (CC2), 1 hank
Color 841 Moss (CC3), 1 hank
Color 836 Pink Ice (CC4), 1 hank
Color 813 Blue Velvet (CC5), 1 hank
Color 819 Chocolate (CC6), 1 hank
Color 801 Army Green (CC7) 1 hank

Needles

Size 4 (3.5 mm) straight and 24" circulars
Size 5 (3.75 mm) straight

Notions

9 (9, 8, 8, 10) 5/8" buttons, stitch marker, Stitch holder or scrap yarn, tapestry needle, scissors
Cardigan shown used Dill Buttons style number 201138, color 11 (dillbuttons.com).

Gauge

25 stitches, 33 rows = 4" (10 cm) in stockinette stitch on larger needles

175, 18)" from beg, ending on a WS row.

Shape cap: BO 4 (5, 4, 5, 4) sts at beg of next two rows, then (BO 2 sts at beg of next 2 rows, BO 1 st at beg of following 2 rows) 6 (6, 7, 7, 8) times. BO 1 st at beg of next two rows. BO 3 sts at beg of next 4 rows. BO rem 16 (18, 18, 20, 20) sts.

Right front

Using smaller straight needles and MC, CO 51 (55, 59, 63, 67) sts.

Row 1 (RS): K3, (p2, k2) across.
Row 2 (WS): (P2, k2) until 2 sts rem, p3.
Rep rows 1 and 2 until ribbing measures 2" from beg, ending with a WS row.
Change to larger needles and work 2 rows in st st.
Join CC1 and work 2 rows in st st.
Cut CC1 and resume using MC, working first dec row for waist shaping as follows: k until 3 sts rem, k2tog, k1.
Work even in st st and rep dec row every 18th row 2 times.
Work 1" even in st st ending on a WS, then work first inc row: K until 1 st rem, M1L, k1.
Work even in st st and rep inc row every 18th row 2 times.
Work 18 (18, 20, 22, 22) rows even.
Begin armhole shaping (WS): BO 4 (5, 4, 5, 4) sts, purl to end.
Knit one row.
Next row: BO 2 sts, purl to end.
Knit one row.
Next row: BO 1 st, purl to end.
Rep last two rows three more times; 41 (44, 49, 52, 57) sts rem.
Work 30 (32, 32, 34, 36) rows even, ending on a WS row.
Shape neck (RS): BO 7 (7, 8, 8, 9) sts, k to end.
Purl 1 row.
Next row: BO 3 sts, k to end.
Purl 1 row.
Next row: BO 2 sts, k to end.
Purl 1 row.
Rep last two rows 1 (2, 2, 3, 3) time(s) more.
Next row: BO 1 st, k to end.
Purl 1 row.
Rep last two rows 4 (5, 5, 6, 6) more times. 22 sts rem.
Knit 1 row.

Shape shoulders (WS): BO 6 (6, 7, 7, 8) sts, p to end.
Knit one row.
Rep last two rows once more.
Next row: BO 5 (5, 6, 6, 7) sts, p to end.
Knit one row.
Rep last two rows once more; all sts bound off. Cut yarn.

Left front

Work as for right front, reversing all shaping and substituting ssk for k2tog decreases.

Back

Using smaller straight needles and MC, CO 110 (118, 126, 134, 142) sts.
Row 1 (RS): K2, (p2, k2) across.
Row 2: (WS): P2, (k2, p2) across.
Rep rows 1 and 2 until ribbing measures 2" from beg, ending with a WS row.
Change to larger needles and work 2 rows in st st.
Join CC1 and work 2 rows in st st.
Cut CC1 and resume using MC, working first dec row for waist shaping as follows: k1, ssk, k until 3 sts rem, k2tog, k1.
Work even in st st and rep dec row every 18th row 2 times.
Work 1" even in st st ending on a WS, then work first inc row: K1, M1R, k until 1 st rem, M1L, k1.
Work even in st st and rep inc row every 18th row 2 times.
Work 18 rows even, ending on a RS.
Begin armhole shaping: BO 4 (5, 4, 5, 4) sts at beg of next 2 rows, 2 sts at beg of following 2 rows, then 1 st at beg of next 8 rows. 90 (96, 106, 112, 122) sts rem.
Purl 1 row.
Continuing to work even in st st using MC and CC1–4, begin Bluebird Chart as follows: K 50 (56, 66, 72, 82) sts, pm, work chart over rem 40 sts.
Once chart is complete, work even until back measures same as fronts to beg of shoulder shaping.
Shape shoulders: BO 6 (6, 7, 7, 8) sts at beg of next 4 rows, then 5 (5, 6, 6, 7) sts at beg of following 4 rows.
Leave rem 46 (52, 54, 60, 62) sts on a holder for neck band.

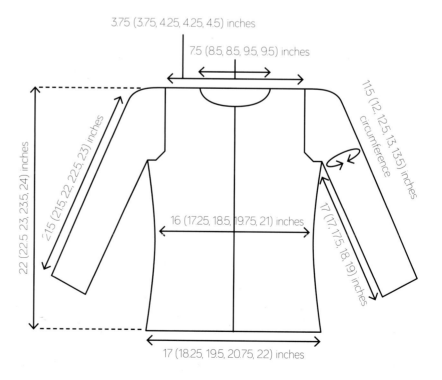

3.75 (3.75, 4.25, 4.25, 4.5) inches

7.5 (8.5, 8.5, 9.5, 9.5) inches

11.5 (12, 12.5, 13, 13.5) inches circumference

22 (22.5, 23, 23.5, 24) inches

21.5 (21.5, 22, 22.5, 23) inches

16 (17.25, 18.5, 19.75, 21) inches

17 (17, 17.5, 18, 19) inches

17 (18.25, 19.5, 20.75, 22) inches

INTARSIA COLORWORK

Step 1: When preparing to change colors, drop current working yarn to the left, draping over new working yarn.

Step 2: Pick up new working yarn and begin knitting or purling as usual. By picking it up from underneath the previous working yarn, a twist has occurred. This twist will prevent a hole from forming at the color change.

Step 3: Continue working until the next color section begins and repeat steps one and two. Each new section of color requires a new strand of yarn, even if the color is in use a few stitches away.

Finishing

Weave in ends from Bluebird chart. Using CC5-7 with finished photographs as a guide, embroider embellishments onto bluebird, flowers, leaves, and branches.

Seam shoulders together, then set in sleeves. Sew side seams and arm seams.

Work buttonbands: Begin on left front to work buttonband side first. With RS facing and using smaller circular needles and MC, pick up 131 (131, 143, 143, 147) sts.

Row 1 (WS): Work in (p2, k2) rib until 3 sts rem; p3. Row 2 (RS): K3, (p2, k2) across. Rep last two rows 3 more times, then BO all sts in pattern.

Move to right front and work huttonhole side, either as follows or using buttonband side to plan your own buttonhole placement: With RS facing, using smaller circular needles and MC, pick up 131 (131, 143, 143, 147) sts.

Row 1 (WS): P3, (k2, p2) across.

Row 2 (RS): Work in (k2, p2) rib until 3 st rem, k3.

Rep last two rows once more.

Sizes 34, 36.5 and 44 only: Next row (WS): P3, *(k2, p2) 3 times, yo, k2tog, p2*, rep from * to * 7 (7, -, -, 8) times; 8 (8, -, -, 9) buttonholes made.

Sizes 39 and 41.5 only: Next row (WS): P3, *(k2, p2) 4 times, yo, k2tog, p2*, rep from * to * - (-, 6, 6, -) times; - (-, 7, 7, -) buttonholes made. Final buttonhole for all sizes will be made in collar.

Work 3 more rows even in ribbing as established, ending on RS. BO all sts in pattern.

Collar: With RS facing and beg at bound off edge of buttonhole band (right front), pick up and knit 32 (35, 36, 39, 40) sts along right front neck edge, k across held sts from back neck, then pick up and knit 32 (35, 36, 39, 40) sts along left front neck to bound off edge of buttonband. 110 (122, 126, 138, 142) sts.

Row 1 (WS): P2, (k2, p2) across.

Row 2 (RS): K2, (p2, k2) across.

Buttonhole row: P2, (k2, p2) to last 4 sts, yo, k2tog, p2.

Work 5 more rows even even in rib pattern as established, ending on RS.

BO all sts in pattern. Weave in ends and block sweater to finished measurements.

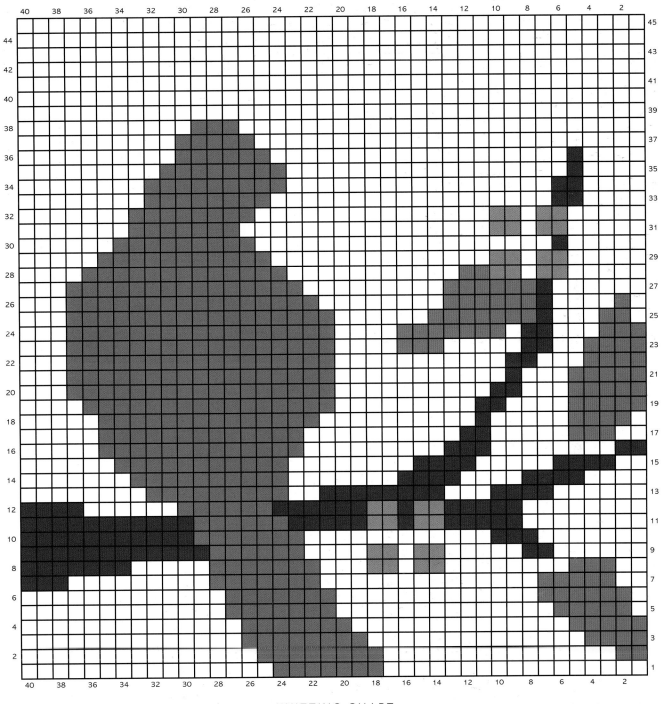

KNITTING CHART

Household

Hummingbird Coffee Cozy

Partridge Holiday Pillow

Magpie Ring Pillow

Hummingbird Coffee Cozy

Hummingbirds flit and feed around this bright and whimsical coffee cozy, perfect for grabbing a cup to go. A wonderful gift idea for eco-minded friends!

Notes

- Cozy is worked in the round with RS facing throughout pattern. It is designed to fit snugly, and will stretch out slightly with use.
- Position MC to be worked in the right hand, CC in the left hand. This will ensure that the CC appears visually dominant, allowing the birds and plants to pop!
- Secure floats of unused color on WS of work every 5–6 sts, taking care to secure in different locations for each round to avoid gutters.
- On rounds using only one color, drop unused color and allow to hang at back of work. Loosely carry it up on the WS to use again on later rounds. This will create a vertical float on the back of the work.

Glossary of abbreviations

BO – bind off
CC – contrast color
CO – cast on
m – marker, markers
M1L – make one left increase: insert right hand needle under bar between stitches from front to back; knit through back loop.

M1R – make one right increase: insert right hand needle under bar between stitches from back to front; knit through front loop.
MC – main color
pm – place marker
RS – right side
sts – stitches
WS – wrong side

Finished Size

9" circumference at widest point, 4" high (unstretched); suitable for 12–20 oz disposable coffee cup.

Yarn

Cascade 220 Sport (100% Peruvian Highland Wool; 164 yd [150 m] 50g): color 8910 Citron (MC) 1 hank; color 9570 Concord Grape (CC) 1 hank.

Needles

Size 3 (3.25 mm) double pointed

Notions

1 marker (m), tapestry needle, scissors

Gauge

29 sts and 37 rounds = 4" (10 cm) in charted pattern

Cozy

Using long tail method and CC, CO 56 sts. PM and join to begin working in the round.

Rounds 1–3: (K2, P2) around.

Round 4: Join MC and begin chart.

On chart rounds 8, 16, 24, and 32, work increases as follows: K1, M1L, work in chart pattern until 1 st remains, M1R, k1. Keep increases in MC throughout.

Once chart is complete, cut MC yarn and knit one round in CC. Work two rounds in k2, p2 rib, then BO in pattern.

Cut yarns and weave in ends on WS, taking care to weave MC ends into MC sts and CC ends into CC sts. Block to finished measurements.

M1L: Make one left increase: insert right hand needle from front to back under bar between stitches.

M1R: Make one right increase: insert right hand needle from back to front under bar between stitches.

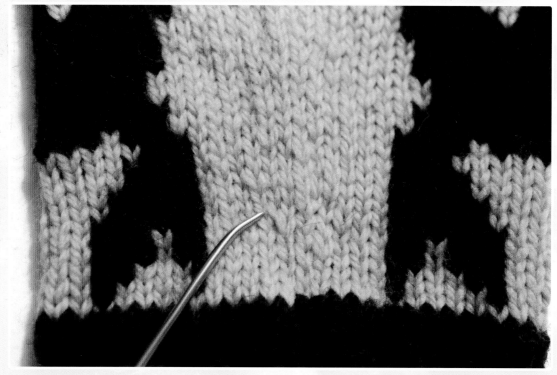

The M1L increase indicated blends in with the knit stitches around it, and is virtually invisible.

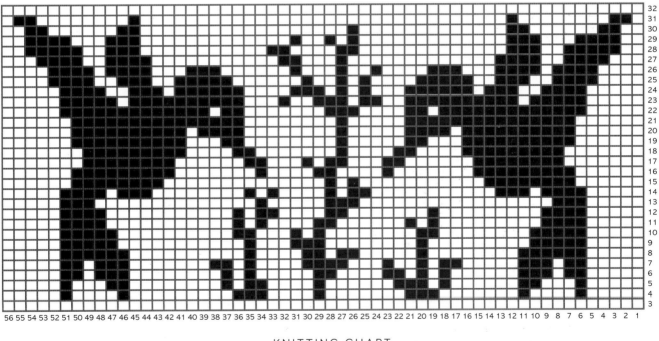

KNITTING CHART

KEY

□ = k with MC

■ = k with CC

Partridge Holiday Pillow

On the first day of Christmas... decorate your home with this traditional colorwork pillow! Creamy white and cranberry red add just the right touch of old-fashioned holiday cheer to any room.

Notes

- Take care to leave a long tail at the cast on edge to use for seaming the bottom of the pillow when knitting is completed. This will help to minimize finishing!
- Note that front and back charts are divided by a purl stitch worked in MC.

Pillow

Using MC, CO 152 sts. PM and join to begin knitting in the round. Beginning with Partridge Chart, work across row 1, p1 in MC, pm, work across row 1 of Branches Chart, p1 in MC. Continue as established until charted rounds are complete, cutting CC after round 90; do not bind off.

Button band flap

Purl across first 75 sts, then BO rem 77 sts knitwise. Note: You must knit two stitches before the first bind off stitch can be worked to preserve the full 75 purl stitches just worked. When bind off is completed, slip last BO st from right hand needle to left hand needle as if to purl, then k2tog.

Finished Size

14" wide, 16" long including button band flap after blocking

Yarn

Cascade 220 (100% Peruvian Highland Wool; 220 yd [200 m] 100g): color 8884 Claret (MC) 1 hank; color 8010 Natural (CC) 2 hanks.

Needles

Size 7 (4.5mm) 24" circular

Notions

2 stitch markers (m), tapestry needle, scissors, 14" square pillow form, 3 1" buttons. Pillow shown used 14" form by Soft n Crafty (joann.com), bone buttons from Renaissance Buttons (renaissancebuttons.com)

Gauge

21 stitches, 26 rounds = 4" (10 cm) in stranded pattern

Glossary of abbreviations

BO – bind off
CC – contrast color
CO – cast on
inc – increase, increasing
k – knit
m – marker, markers
MC – main color
p – purl
rem – remaining
rep – repeat
pm – place marker
RS – right side
st, sts – stitch, stitches
WS – wrong side

Step 1: With right side of work facing and working from right to left across bottom opening, insert yarn needle under the point of the knit stitch on the top piece,

Begin working back and forth on rem 75 sts in MC for button flap as follows:

Ribbing Setup Row: K2, P2 across, inc 3 sts evenly (78 sts).

Row 1 (RS): K2, (p2, k2) across.

Row 2 (WS): P2, (k2, p2) across.

Rep rows 1 and 2 for a total of 8 rows.

Row 9 (RS): Work 15 sts in established rib pattern, (BO next 4 sts, work 17 sts in pattern) twice, BO next 4 sts, work rem 14 sts in rib pattern.

Row 10 (WS): Work in ribbing to first BO gap, (CO 4 sts, work in ribbing to next gap) twice, CO 4 sts, work in ribbing to end.

Rep rows 1 and 2 for 8 more rows.

BO in rib pattern, cut yarn.

Finishing

Using long tail from cast on edge and mattress stitch, sew up bottom opening of pillow cover. Sew on three buttons on pillow cover back, aligning them with buttonholes on ribbed flap.

Block to finished measurements and when dry, insert pillow form and button flap closed.

Step 2: then under the point of the knit stitch on the bottom piece. Repeat these steps across the opening, moving from top to bottom piece and working one stitch at a time.

Step 3: While working mattress stitch, check to make sure the front and back of pillow cover are aligned correctly. The vertical lines in the border pattern are a great indicator!

PARTRIDGE KNITTING CHART

BRANCHES KNITTING CHART

Magpie Ring Pillow

Long a symbol of cheer, good fortune, and the arrival of guests, magpies are also beloved for their chatty nature and sweeping tails. Their striking black, white, and blue markings are captured here in a smooth silk blend yarn embellished with sparkling glass beads. The Magpie Ring Pillow is sure to bring a touch of whimsy and luck to any wedding!

Notes

- Pillow front and back are knit separately and seamed.
- Magpie motif is added after knitting using duplicate stitch technique.
- Consider embroidering the name of the couple or wedding date in the space surrounding the birds for a special memento.

Glossary of abbreviations

CC – contrast color
CO – cast on
MC – main color
RS – right side

st st – stockinette stitch
sts – stitches
WS – wrong side

Pillow front/back (make two)

Using MC, CO 66 sts and work in st st until piece measures 8.25" long.
Bind off all sts and weave in ends on WS. Block both pieces to 8.25" square.

Finishing

Following Magpie Chart and using CC and duplicate stitch method, add birds to pillow front. Weave in all ends on WS, taking care to weave CC ends in behind birds so they will not show on RS.

With WS held together and using mattress stitch, seam 3 sides of pillow closed. Insert pillow form and seam final side; secure yarn and cut. Thread sewing needle with black thread and using photo of finished pillow and step-by-step photos as a guide, add cascades of cobalt teardrops to four corners. Thread sewing needle with white thread and edge pillow in hematite beads.
Attach satin ribbon if desired to hold rings on pillow during ceremony.

Finished Size

Pillow measures 8" square, not including bead embellishments.

Yarn

Cascade Heritage Silk (85% Superwash Merino Wool, 15% Mulberry Silk; 437 yd [400 m] 100 g): color 5618 Snow (MC), 1 hank; color 5672 Real Black (CC), 1 hank.

Needles

Size 3 (3.25 mm) straight

Notions

Approx. 10 grams size 6/0 hematite beads, 1 strand of royal blue teardrop beads, 8" square pillow form, Black ¼" satin ribbon, black and white sewing thread, sewing needle to fit through beads, tapestry needle, scissors.

Pillow shown used 8" form from Deb Madir Designs (debmadirdesigns.com); Beader's Paradise Czech glass beads in Hematite LT6E10 (beadersparadiseonline.com); Advantus Corp small teardrop beads in Royal SUL50967 (shopadvantus.com for locations).

Gauge

31 stitches, 40 rows = 4" (10 cm) in stockinette stitch

Step 1: Bring yarn through the base of the stitch from the WS, then working on surface of the fabric, from right to left around the base of the stitch above.

Step 2: Complete the duplicate stitch by taking needle to WS of work at the base of the stitch in the same place as the beginning. Take care not to pull too tightly; duplicate stitches should sit atop knitted stitches.

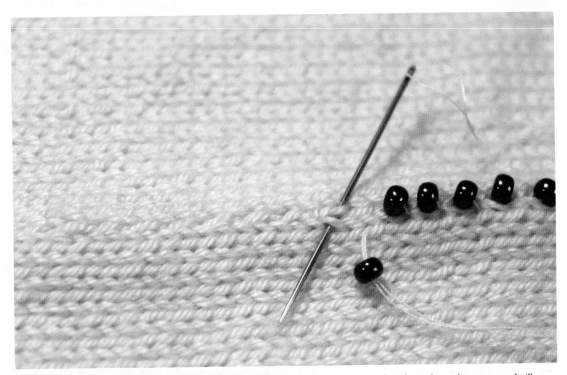

Step 3: Beginning in a corner and using white sewing thread, whip stitch hematite beads in place along seam of pillow.

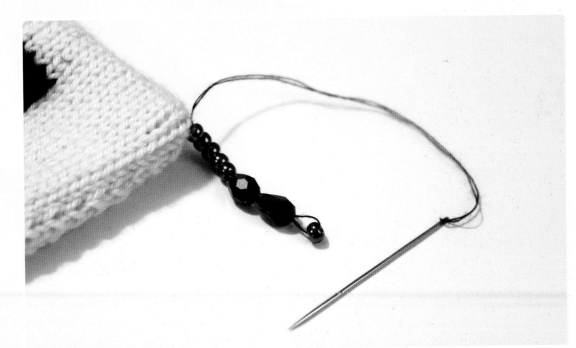

Step 4: Using black sewing thread, attach cascades of teardrop beads to four corners of pillow as follows: anchor sewing thread to pillow corner, then thread on between 2–7 hematite beads and 1–3 teardrops. Add 1 more hematite bead beneath the teardrops, then double back through the previous beads and secure to pillow corner. Final hematite bead will keep the other beads locked in place.

84
82
80
78
76
74
72
70
68
66
64
62
60
58
56
54
52
50
48
46
44
42
40
38
36
34
32
30
28
26
24
22
20
18
16
14
12
10
8
6
4
2

66 64 62 60 58 56 54 52 50 48 46 44 42 40 38 36 34 32 30 28 26 24 22 20 18 16 14 12 10 8 6 4 2

KNITTING CHART

KEY

☐ = knit with MC   ■ = duplicate stitch with CC

Acknowledgments

Thank you so much to my wonderful family and friends. This book would not have been possible without your endless support and encouragement! Thank you to my amazing husband John Ostrander for his boundless faith in me and his incredible patience and keen eye during the hours of how-to photography. Thank you to my parents, Alan Young and Ava Scott, for wearing so many hats: cheerleaders, editors, photographers, stylists, think tank. I love you! Thank you to my beautiful sister and friends for modeling my creations, stomping through snow and smiling despite it all: Hannah Young, Jessica Melber, Nick Leuthauser, Lark Barnett, Kelly Kurposka, Jen Heinlein, Season Gillberg, and Anli Hu. Thank you to my speedy test knitter and fabulous friend Gretchen Mashmann. Finally, thank you to my grandmothers Mary Young and Judith Scott, to whom I owe my passion, determination, and creativity.

Special thanks as well to Robena DeMatteo and Ruth Rich of Trumpet Hill, Jen Heinlein of Sage Yarn, Jo Bryant of BlueRed Press, Shannon Dunbabin of Cascade Yarns, and Sandy Powers of Cape Cod Crochet. Your generosity and guidance mean the world to me.

3 1901 05424 9182